When Congress
Makes a Joke

When Congress Makes a Joke

Congressional Humor Then and Now

Dean L. Yarwood

ROWMAN & LITTLEFIELD PUBLISHERS, INC.
Lanham • Boulder • New York • Toronto • Oxford

ROWMAN & LITTLEFIELD PUBLISHERS, INC.

Published in the United States of America
by Rowman & Littlefield Publishers, Inc.
A wholly owned subsidiary of The Rowman & Littlefield Publishing Group, Inc.
4501 Forbes Boulevard, Suite 200, Lanham, Maryland 20706
www.rowmanlittlefield.com

PO Box 317, Oxford OX2 9RU, UK

British Library Cataloguing in Publication Information Available

Library of Congress Cataloging-in-Publication Data

Yarwood, Dean L.
  When Congress makes a joke: congressional humor then and now / Dean L.
Yarwood.
    p. cm.
  Includes bibliographical references and index.
  ISBN 0-7425-3042-6 (cloth :alk. paper) — ISBN 0-7425-3043-4 (paper: alk. paper)
  1. United States—Politics and government—Humor. 2. Legislators—United
States—Humor. 3. United States. Congress—Humor. 4. Legislators—United
States—Biography. 5. United States. Congress—Biography. 6. American wit and
humor. I. Title.
  PN6231.P6Y37 2004
  328.73'002'07—dc22

                                                                                2004000944

Printed in the United States of America

♾ ™ The paper used in this publication meets the minimum requirements of
American National Standard for Information Sciences—Permanence of Paper
for Printed Library Materials, ANSI/NISO Z39.48-1992.

Dedicated to the memory of my parents,
Harold and Elsie Yarwood

Contents

Preface

The 2002 off-year elections were swirling about me as I was completing this book. On the campaign trail, Senator Jean Carnahan (D-MO) commented "I'm the number one target of the White House. Since they can't get Osama bin Laden, they're going to get me." The comment ended up on CNN and brought indignant protests from state Republicans. They fired off a press release calling her comment "despicable" and "a slap at the armed forces fighting in Afghanistan" (J. Berger 2002, A2). Even though the Missouri senate race had in fact been targeted by national Republicans, she nonetheless felt compelled to issue an apology (Mannies 2002, A2). But why? What is there about humor that makes politicians feel as though they need to back off from humorous remarks even if, as in this case, they are a means of communicating a valid message?

Senator John McCain (R-AZ), a maverick within his party, told a tasteless joke involving the Clinton family and Janet Reno while addressing a Republican fund-raiser. He quickly realized his error and sent a note of apology to President Clinton. In an interview with political columnist Maureen Dowd, he acknowledged that his joke was "stupid and cruel and insensitive" (Dowd 1998, B7; see also, Victor 1998, 1508). As interesting as the incident was, as well as the senator's reaction to it, what is more interesting is the interpretation offered by a noted student of humor, anthropologist Alan Dundes. He commented that if McCain was worried about being perceived as too liberal, this was one way to be "one of the Republican boys—attacking the Democratic President by attacking his women. Since ancient times, you get at your male opponent by violating his women. If the women's honor is lost, the man's honor is lost. McCain was in the military. He knows you conquer enemies by feminizing the men and putting down the women" (as cited in Dowd 1998, B7). Would Senator McCain agree that what he really intended to do was vanquish the president by dishonoring his women? Perhaps. But the incident raises a couple of noteworthy questions: first, How many levels does humor have? and second, Is the humor's creator responsible for the meanings that attach but were never consciously intended?

At least two cabinet members during the last quarter-century have driven the final nails into their political coffins by attempting to use racial and ethnic humor. While campaigning, President Ford's secretary of agriculture, Earl Butz, told a racially insensitive story to a private group that included a *Rolling Stone* reporter and somehow didn't expect it to get out. It did, and he was out of his job. He had previously apologized for a joke in which he imitated an Italian woman with a heavy accent who, in reference to the Pope's position regarding birth control, commented, "He no playa da game: he no maka da rules" (Robbins 1976, 1, 32).

President Reagan's secretary of the interior, James G. Watt, was continually in and out of controversy for several offhanded remarks that tickled some but upset others. He made a hasty departure from office after he offered what he thought was a lighthearted description of the balance on a coal advisory commission: "I have a black, I have a woman, two Jews, and a cripple. And we have talent" (Shabecoff 1983, 1).

These various incidents demonstrate that humor in politics is an unstable element and can blow up in one's face, causing inestimable damage. It is a kind of play that can lead to unpredictable outcomes, even ones that end public careers. Innumerable cases of humor-gone-wrong make perhaps even most members of Congress humor-adverse. Then again, most of them arguably do not see the humor in politics because, for them, politics is deadly serious—it has a specific gravity, making the profession a weighty affair.

At the same time, some politicians have been able to use humor as a valued tool to enhance their stature. Presidents Kennedy and Reagan come to mind as leaders who were known for their ready use of humor. Members of the press would wait for their witticisms, and, as a result, these presidents may have gotten a "pass" from the press in cases where their presidential actions should have been subjected to hard analysis. In Congress, we need look no further than the careers of Senators Alben Barkley and Sam Ervin and Representative Morris Udall to find members who used humor effectively in their legislative work. They drew on it to deflate tense situations, bring members together, and show themselves as members who were so confident of their mastery of the language that they could play with words and ideas to enhance their effectiveness. All in all, their humor, while often reinforcing norms of the institution, gave evidence that these public servants were accepted members of their respective legislative bodies.

In this book, I focus on the public humor of congressional members, from the beginning of Congress to the present. To do so, not only do I rely on the autobiographies of former members who are noted for their use of humor, but I also cite the published works of other former members who, though not noted for their use of humor, nonetheless show an appreciation for its importance. I also draw on the works of historians who write on the topic of humor in Congress and other books which feature the collected humor of Congress. In addition, I have conducted personal interviews with contemporary members of the House and Senate. In each case, I have sought to allow congressional members to tell us, in their own words, about the various facets of humor: how it is created, how it is used, and what the perceived consequences are. It is their world, and it is their understanding of congressional humor that I present in this book.

While the focus is on the public humor of members of Congress, another type of study has gained much acceptance over the years. It is the witty insights offered by astute outsiders that portray Congress as it often appears to the public. This includes the humor of Artemus Ward, Mark Twain, and Will Rogers, among others. Their view of Congress varies widely from that of the members on whom we draw—in these humorists, we see the simple logic of common sense confronting the convoluted and tortured outcomes of congressional compromises. I employ these perspectives as epigraphs at the head of each chapter for no other reason than to cite them for the sharp contrast they present to the humor of members, a humor that barely conceals their awe of the institution.

In pursuing my interest in elite humor as it has manifested itself in the U.S. Congress, I have received assistance from many sources. I have been helped immensely by a generous grant from the University of Missouri Research Board. It would have been difficult to go forward with this work without its support. Among other objectives, it has enabled me to employ some very able research assistants, including Matthew Eshbaugh-Sola, who transcribed the phone interviews and assisted me with several chapters; Michael Middleton, who provided valuable assistance with chapter 4; and Kimberly Beecham, who gathered data of interest from documentary sources.

A number of my colleagues read portions of this manuscript and offered useful suggestions regarding its earlier renderings. They include Gary Young, James Endersby, and KC Morrison. I am grateful for their helpful insights.

I am especially grateful to Representatives Barney Frank, W. G. "Bill" Hefner, Henry Hyde, and Patricia Schroeder; and to Senators Dale Bumpers, Conrad Burns, Robert Dole, Pat Roberts, and Allen K. Simpson, for taking time out of their busy schedules to speak with me about humor in Congress.

Parts of chapters 2 and 6 appear in *Humor: International Journal of Humor Research* (14, no. 4, published by Mouton de Gruyter). An earlier version of chapter 3 appears in *Administration and Society* (35, no. 1, published by Sage Publications).

ACKNOWLEDGMENTS

I wish to thank the following for giving permission to use quotations:

From *That Reminds Me*, by Alben W. Barkley, copyright © 1954 by Alben W. Barkley. Used by permission of Doubleday, a division of Random House, Inc.

From *Congressional Anecdotes*, by Paul F. Boller Jr., copyright © 1992 by Paul F. Boller, Jr. Used by permission of Oxford University Press, Inc.

Reprinted from *Humor of a Country Lawyer*, by Sam J. Ervin Jr., copyright © 1983 by Sam J. Ervin Jr. Used by permission of the University of North Carolina Press.

Reprinted with the permission of Simon & Schuster Adult Publishing Group, from *Fishbait: The Memoirs of the Congressional Doorkeeper*, by William "Fishbait" Miller as told to Frances S. Leighton. Copyright © 1977 by William Moseley Miller and Frances Spatz Leighton.

From *24 Years of House Work . . . and the Place Is Still a Mess*, copyright © 1998 by Pat Schroeder, reprinted with permission of Andrews McMeel, Publishing. All rights reserved.

From *Too Funny to Be President*, by Morris K. Udall, copyright © 1988 by Morris K. Udall. Reprinted by permission of the Henry Holt and Company, LLC.

From *As I Knew Them*, by James E. Watson, The Bobbs-Merrill Company, 1936. Copyright © 1964 Joseph Cannon Watson, reprinted by permission of Deborah Watson.

1

Speaking Humor to Power

But with Congress, every time they make a joke it's a law. And every time they make a law it's a joke.

—Will Rogers

In his presidential address delivered before the Twenty-first Meeting of the American Political Science Association in New York City on December 28, 1926, President Charles E. Merriam admonished his colleagues, "It sometimes seems that we political scientists take ourselves and our subject too soberly. . . . No one of us has ever even written a dissertation on the important function of humor in political affairs" (Merriam 1926, 5). He could as well have saved his breath—three-quarters of a century later, the discipline has yet to approach the study of political humor and how humor leavens or acerbates political affairs.

This inattention is in spite of the fact that most practicing politicians see humor as central to their work and as deadly serious when used in political discussions. One astute commentator writes, "Political humor is a very serious business. It's so serious that every 1988 presidential campaign will spend considerable effort, energy, and time proving that its candidate possesses a well-rounded sense of humor" (Shields 1987, 15). Shields needn't have confined his comments to the 1988 campaigns, for another political observer puts the case even stronger: "Humor is the nitroglycerin of political speech. It is a substance of great power when handled properly; mishandled, it can explode with fatal consequences" (Greenfield 1980, 124). If politicians are good at using it, then they know they have a gift. If they are not, then they carefully avoid using it in their

1

work, although they may enjoy the humor of their colleagues or they might employ a professional gag writer to compensate for their lack of innate wittiness.

In this book, I consider the humor of political elites, specifically, members of the U.S. Congress. Although their humor might be either public or private, I am primarily concerned with their public utterances. The humor that interests me is generally encompassed in the terms *mirth* and *wit*. Types of humor within this purview include, but are not confined to, those that are occasioned by surprising or incongruent shifts of thoughts, exaggeration, word play, repartee, irony, satire, ridicule, and sarcasm when employed by political elites in their public lives. I am not concerned with the politically relevant humor of late-night talk-show hosts, stand-up comedians, or political cartoonists—enjoyable as these forms of humor may be. These latter forms of humor come from critics of the show, not from the actors on the political stage, though admittedly actors feel the roasting they get from the critics, and critics get their fuel from the show.

IMPORTANT UNDERSTANDINGS REGARDING HUMOR

Humor and laughter are often thought to be synonymous. Many scholars of humor seem to have made this association that laughter and humor naturally go together as thunder and lightning or as SUVs and gas. In fact, laughter is a type of universal communication that seems to have developed early in the history of *Homo sapiens* and is tied to a range of human behaviors other than humor. These are some of the conclusions that neuroscientist Robert Provine has drawn in a recent book dealing with laughter (2000, chaps. 3, 5). Some of his findings result from sending researchers into malls to eavesdrop on patterns of laughter that occur in conversations between shoppers. In all, he analyzes twelve hundred "laugh episodes." What he finds is that speakers laugh more often than their audiences (46 percent more), and most interesting, "most laughter did not follow anything resembling a joke, storytelling, or other formal attempt at humor" (27, 40). Only 10 to 20 percent of the comments that occasioned the laughter are even remotely humorous. What do people laugh at? Such mundane comments as "I'll see you guys later," "We can handle this," "I told you so," and "Must be nice" (40). These are more like the utterances of humans waiting for answers to such questions as "Do you think I am okay?" "Is my response acceptable?" "Are we in agreement?" than responses to the presentations of great wits. Another scholar of humor writes about the several messages of humor: "People laugh to get over moments of social awkwardness, to indicate deference, or to give evidence that the situation is amicable" (P. Berger 1997, 39).

This brings us to the second understanding of our subject: Humor is social behavior. People seldom laugh when they are alone, and what they laugh about is funny to them because of the humor's socially derived meanings. This point is made by the philosopher Henri Bergson in his important essay "Laughter." Concerned with the comic aspects of laughter, he writes, "The comic does not exist outside the pale of what is strictly *human*. A landscape may be beautiful, charming and sublime, or insignificant and ugly; it will never be laughable" ([1900] 1956, 62 [emphasis in original]). He goes on to comment that laughter needs an echo and that "our laughter is always the laughter of a group" (64). Noted anthropologist Mary Douglas asserts, "The social dimension enters at all levels of the perception of a joke" (Douglas 1975, 97). Along the same lines, Gary Fine writes that in researching humor "the sociologist typically examines the social context of humor. . . . At the very least the context must implicitly be taken into account. This increases the difficulty of research. No longer can humorous stimuli be given to individual subjects, but rather the social forces that influence the creation and appreciation of humor must be considered" (Fine 1983, 159). Relevant to the importance of social context, Dutch sociologist Anton C. Zijderveld points out that "humour and laughter often mark the boundaries of a group" and that "humour withers away when it is separated, for whatever reason from its original cultural and social matrix" (Zijderveld 1983, 47, 49). The meaning of humor is based on interpretations shared by group members; humor identifies members of the group and is a source of group cohesion; and it often is useful in defining relationships between groups (see also P. Berger 1997, chap. 5; Martineau 1972).

One finding that receives support in the literature is that one's position in the group affects one's humor. There is a tendency for joking relationships to be symmetrical, that is, between equals; but when it is asymmetrical, the superior in the relationship typically can make jokes at the expense of the subordinate—but not visa versa. This pattern is common in formal organizations (see Bradney 1957; Coser 1960; Lundberg 1969; Traylor 1985). For example, in her study of a psychiatric hospital, Rose Coser finds that "the most frequent targets of the senior staff were junior members; the humor of the latter was more frequently directed against patients and their relatives, as well as themselves" (1960, 85). One's status is important not only in determining how much one laughs but also in what circumstances. Provine points out that, while in an executive position, a leader of an organization is likely to avoid either using humor or laughing very much, but as the leader's context changes, he or she may be a barrel of laughs—for example, when drinking with friends or old classmates, or when clowning around with the family (2000, 29–30).

A final useful understanding for our study is an appreciation for the role that marginality plays in humor, just as it does in politics. For instance, in politics, actors who are subjected to conflicting pressures are especially important role players. As managers of bureaus, they may be former professionals who have shifted to management; it is very much their responsibility to moderate between the clash of management and professional values. In legislatures, members who are subjected to conflicting pressures are more likely to shift as coalitions form and disintegrate. Voters who are subjected to cross pressures are more likely to shift their allegiances, and so on. These marginal political actors see a more complicated world and understand more viewpoints than their unconflicted brethren.

Marginality is also important in humor that often depends on the ability to stand outside the mainstream of society and see relationships that elude those who are better integrated. Those who are in the mainstream share worldviews that are socially derived, and they may feel deeply threatened when their assumed institutions seem to evidence slippage or when their deeply held values are challenged. Marginal people do not share in the social cohesion of mainstream groups and may perceive the world with a more detached, analytical perspective. In some instances, they may harbor some suspicion toward a society of which they are on the outside or only partially integrated into. They are in a better position to imagine alternate social arrangements, and they may even view the status quo with some bemusement. Peter Berger writes about the relationship between marginality and the creation of humor: "The intellectual game of wit is best played from a social margin, be it ascribed (as in the case of Jewish humor) or achieved (as in the case of the dandy qua sardonic observer). The marginalization, though, is strangely dialectical. The marginal individual, through the magic of his wit, in turn marginalizes the world that he targets. It is now no longer *the* world, but *a* world—and a ridiculous one at that. This marginalization— or one could say, relativization—of the world is what makes wit dangerous, potentially subversive, even if the individual practicing it has no such thing in mind" (P. Berger 1997, 152, emphasis in original). In America, persons of Jewish background have been especially represented among professional comedians. Avner Ziv estimates that at one time, almost 80 percent of the most successful humorists were Jewish, in spite of the fact that Jews make up only 3 percent of the U.S. population (as cited in A. A. Berger 1993, 93–94). Other marginal groups as well— ethnic, racial, and religious—have produced stand-up comics who poke fun at mainstream society's hang-ups and sometimes at the groups of which they are a member.

THEORIES OF HUMOR

It is common in discussions of humor to identify three theories of humor: superiority humor, the humor of incongruity, and relief humor (see, for example, Berlyne 1969, 799–803; Morreall 1987, ix, 5–6). Of these, the former two types have occasioned the most discussion.

On the surface, the superiority theory of humor would seem to be the most akin to the interests of political science students, given their concern with power and its use. It can be raucous humor in which the victors humiliate their opponents and, in turn, may find themselves humbled. With superiority humor, the heat of ridicule would seem to be fueled by the passion of politics. For example, one prominent scholar of political humor writes that political humor is a form of sublimated aggression: "Humor provides a socially acceptable release of repressed emotions of our primitive aggressiveness. Politics as a war of words is then an arena in which humor is indispensable for limiting the war to words. And, because wordplay is the essence of much humor, the political arena will be the natural abode of the bon mot, particularly as comic invective" (Schutz 1977a, 8, 25).

The origins of superiority humor have been traced to the ancient Greeks and Romans, including Plato, Aristotle, and Cicero (P. Berger 1997, chap. 2; Koestler 1997, 683; and Morreall 1987, 10–18). However, the one who is most often cited in connection with the superiority theory of humor is the English philosopher Thomas Hobbes. The quotation of his that is most often taken as indicative of his thoughts about laughter comes from a discussion of human character found in *The Elements of the Law*, published in 1640: "The passion of laughter is nothing else but a sudden glory arising from sudden conception of some eminency in ourselves, by comparison with the infirmities of others, or with our own formerly" (Hobbes [1640] 1969, 42). Communications scholar Charles Gruner is probably the most unflinching of contemporary students of humor who espouse the superiority theory. In his *Understanding Humor*, he writes, "*Ridicule* is the basic component of all humorous material, and that to *understand* a piece humorous material it is necessary only to find out who is ridiculed, how, and why" (1978, 14, emphasis in original). Gruner makes it clear that for humor to be effective, it must be sudden and preceded by a great deal of tension (30–31, 44). He traces the origin of laughter to our primordial ancestors, to a time in human development that precedes language: "What touched off his nonverbal grunting, facial contortions, muscular dissembling, and breathing irregularities that presaged our modern 'laughter'? Why, one thing that was available to each of our bestial ancestors: *victory*. Success in combat. Usually success in combat with a fellow man. *Sudden* victory. The sudden realization that one has triumphed, that the prize is his, that his opponent is defeated!" (42–43, emphasis in original). For modern *Homo sapiens*, Gruner contends that laughter results from combat on a verbal terrain, accompanied with a great deal of anxiety and tension, with a sudden victory of one combatant over the other. About two decades after the publication of *Understanding Laughter*, Gruner published another book, *The Game of Humor* (1997). In it, he maintains his position that humor is necessarily aggressive, stating succinctly, "*Laughing equals winning*" (8, emphasis in original). Those victories are best that come suddenly: "And getting what we want *suddenly*, as a surprise, exhilarates us far more than receiving the same as a simple matter of course" (8, emphasis in original). A theme that appears in the 1997 volume (as suggested by the title) and that does not play an important part in the 1978 book is that humor is a game. This is a major change in focus: games have rules and boundaries, as well as beginnings and endings. With each new game, the victor is uncertain; people usually do not continue to play games in which they are unevenly matched. Conceptualized as play, humor is less like the jousting of our bestial ancestors and more like a parlor game, with the participants playing word games and moving concepts about, knowing that the stakes are low and enjoying the give-and-take as much as the outcome.

No doubt, much humor has an aggressive edge. That said, a couple of caveats are in order. First, much-too-much is made of the contributions of Thomas Hobbes to the development of superiority humor. No one would be more surprised than Hobbes himself if he were to return to Earth and find that his work is widely cited as a justification for a popular theory of humor, because he most certainly had no intention of writing a treatise on humor. Rather, he wrote during the English Civil War and its aftermath, and to that end, he wrote to justify the need for a strong sovereign if there were to be peace among his countrymen. This was necessary, he contended, because men were created equal so that, in a state of nature, "every man is the Enemy to every man" and, in that natural state, the life of man is "solitary, poore, nasty, brutish, and short" ([1651] 1991, 89). Thus, men contracted with each other and with the sovereign to constitute civil society. To make his case for the need for a social contract, Hobbes early on in the *Leviathan* discusses the natural psychological characteristics of humans that make it necessary to leave the state of nature. One among many characteristics, or "passions" (as he called them), was "sudden glory," which he covers in a short paragraph within a nearly five-hundred page tome. He writes that "*Sudden Glory, is the passion which maketh those Grimaces called* LAUGHTER; *and is caused either by some sudden act of their own which pleaseth them; or by the apprehension of some deformed thing in another, by comparison whereof they suddenly applaud themselves*" ([1651] 1991, 43, emphasis in original). Moreover, a point that has been lost in the litany of successive citations is that Hobbes goes on to make clear in the *Leviathan* that he thinks it is often those who are *weak* and *cowardly themselves* who have need to make fun of the imperfections in others: "And therefore much Laughter at the defects of others, is a signe of Pusillanimity. For of great minds, one of the proper workes is, to help and free others from scorn; and compare themselves onely with the most able" ([1651] 1991, 43). This is hardly the perspective of contemporaries who cite Hobbes to support superiority humor involving the cruelest kinds of ridicule.

Another point that bears comment is that those who espouse the superiority theory of humor seem to argue that the sole purpose of humor is to reveal others' weaknesses and make themselves seem superior by comparison. However, in most cases, humor is likely to have more than one purpose, and humiliation of others may or may not be one of them. In humor theory, it is presumed that in each case there is a source, a message, a target, and an audience. Now, if the specific target is not a part of the communication net and is unaware of the joke, how can it be said that he or she has been humiliated? And how can the source and the audience feel superior by comparison? Might it not be as plausible to infer that in this case the purpose of the joke is to promote social cohesion? If so, laughing would equal social solidarity more so than winning.[1]

The second type of humor, incongruity humor, is characterized by surprise that results from unexpected interruptions of thought—from juxtaposing widely different ideas, taking figurative expressions literally, playing with words, or from the difference between what is expected and what actually happens. This last definition is offered by Arthur Asa Berger, who writes, "The theory that is most widely held nowadays suggests that humor is based on incongruity, on some kind of difference between what people expect and what they get" (1995, 105). Striking a similar theme, Peter Berger writes that humor results from "the incongruity between order and disorder, by the same token, between man, who always seeks order, and the disorderly realities of the empirical world. In other words, the incongruity perceived here discloses a central truth about the human condition: *Man is in a state of comic discrepancy with respect to the order of the universe*" (1997, 34 [emphasis in original]).

Political scientists James E. Combs and Dan Nimmo trace political humor to the incongruity between democracy's pretensions and its reality. For them, political humor results from the discrepancy between (*a*) the myth that, in a democracy, "government is of the people, for the people and by the people"; and (*b*) the real need for political elites who actually rule. In their book *The Comedy of Democracy*, they write, "The comedy of democracy resides in an ironic incongruity that eternally characterizes self-government, always making it less than it could be. . . . The drama of 'rule of the people' plays out over and over again in ignorance of its own comic flaw, the flaw being not so much that democracy doesn't work as that *it never gets tried*. The ultimate irony of democracy is that, as practiced, democracy rests on a flaw: *democracy can only work if it doesn't work, survive and endure only if its principles are violated"* (1996, 18–19, emphasis in original).

French Philosopher Henri Bergson, who wrote one of the most insightful works about humor, is prominently associated with the incongruity theory of humor. He believed that a primary source of humor was to combine human characteristics with machinelike characteristics. In his essay "Laughter," published in 1900, he writes, *"The attitudes, gestures and movements of the human body are laughable in exact proportion as that body reminds us of a mere machine"* and that humor results from *"something mechanical encrusted on the living"* ([1900] 1956, 79, 84, emphasis in original). Humans have natural processes that result in elasticity; the machine is built to repeat itself in mindless repetitions, no matter a change in the stimulus, and when humans act mindlessly like machines, that is laughable (Bergson, 66–67, 97).

Arthur Koestler's name is also associated with the incongruity theory of humor. In his book *The Act of Creation*, he refers to incongruity humor, which he views as being complex because it involves dealing with different planes of thought simultaneously, by the term "bisociation" ([1964] 1989, 35–36). Humor is the result of merging, or the bisociation, of different matrixes of thought. Koestler employs the term "matrix" to mean "any ability, habit, or skill, any pattern of ordered behaviour governed by a *'code'* of fixed rules" (38, emphasis in original). Other terms that he uses interchangeably with "matrix" are "frames of reference," "associative contexts," "codes of behaviour," systems of logic," and "universes of discourse." Thus, to get comical results owing to the unexpected clash between different systems' meanings, one can juxtapose assumptions of different cultures, values of different historical periods (e.g., *A Connecticut Yankee in King Arthur's Court*), different systems of thought (e.g., scientific and religious thought), and different character types (the ponderous political adviser and the fool).[2]

Two prominent scholars who see humor as rooted in incongruity contend that such humor is set off from the "real world." William Fry, in his book *Sweet Madness*, develops the idea of humor as a paradox, which sets it off from the ordinary, workaday world. He begins by discussing the "vicious circle principle" (1963, chap. 7). Consider the following example:

> *The statement below is true.*
> *The statement above is false.*

Which does one believe? It is a circular paradox that keeps reverberating. Another example is the "catch-22" from Joseph Heller's famous World

War II novel of the same name. It has the main character of the novel, Captain Yossarian, talking to Doc Daneeka about getting grounded. Yossarian was told that indeed a pilot would have to be crazy to continue flying combat missions in the face of continuously close brushes with death and that being crazy was sufficient reason to ground him. But as Doc further explained, if the pilot asked to be grounded, it was a sign he was sane and that he would have to continue to fly combat missions. Hence, the paradox—if one rule is followed, the other is invalidated, and vice versa ([1955] 1961, 47). Fry goes on to point out that humor is created by establishing a "play frame": "The frame can be indicated by a voice quality, a body movement or posture, a lifted eyebrow—any of the various things people do to indicate fantasy to one another" (1963, 138). Fry labels this type of communication as "meta-communication," which delivers the message to the audience that what follows is not real (139). The humor that follows in not real, but to be understood and for it to have its effect, it has to be accepted as real. Thus, paradoxes are created within paradoxes until finally there is a sudden break in logic, the punch line, which brings the audience back to reality (143–53). Apart from humor, Fry sees paradoxes in such activities as rituals, dreams, folklore, fantasy, art, drama, and psychotherapy (132).

Peter Berger characterizes humor as an "intrusion" into the normal serious state of the "real world." He cites Alfred Schutz, an early leader of the phenomenology school of sociology, who discusses a world made up of multiple realities, the "paramount reality" of ordinary everyday existence, and other "finite provinces of meaning" (P. Berger 1997, chap. 1, esp. 6–8). To describe these multiple realities, Berger chooses to use the term "islands of experience," among which are intense sexual or esthetic experience; self-contained theoretical speculation, such as pure mathematics; religious experience; and, relevant to our topic, humor (206). As with Fry, the world of humor is entered either by establishing a play frame, such as by the joker's asking, "Have you heard this one?" or by telegraphing the shift to humor through voice intonation or body language (67). Once the humor "island" is established, the assumptions of the ordinary world are suspended and a new set of rules take precedence: "the comic transcends the reality of ordinary, everyday, existence; it posits, however, temporarily, a different reality in which the assumptions and rules of ordinary life are suspended" (205). When the joke is completed and the humorous incongruity is revealed, the jokester returns the audience to the ordinary reality, with phrases such as "now seriously" or "now to return to our main business" or some such transition (68).

Incongruity theory notwithstanding, not all sudden incongruities are humorous. If one is driving down the road and a deer bounds from the side of the road, it will likely seem sudden and incongruous, but it will not be seen as humorous. Indeed, one will likely respond with fear and panic. To take another case, in stage comedy there is no more of a standard comic routine in slapstick than when an actor slips on a banana peel and does a pratfall. It is sudden, it is incongruous, and it makes people laugh. However, when we see the same scene in real life, we are not likely to break up in laughter. The difference? In the real-life pratfall, we are likely to be emotionally involved and have concern about whether the individual has been hurt or has broken any bones. Henri Bergson points out that an absence of feeling usually accompanies laughter: "Indifference is its natural environment, for laughter has no greater foe than emotion" ([1900] 1956, 63). In the former case, the frame is set, we know that what we see is not real; in the latter, the perception we bring to what we see—concern or merriment—is critical in determining whether we feel pity or laugh.

Relief humor is most closely associated with the names of nineteenth-century social Darwinist philosopher Herbert Spencer and psychologist Sigmund Freud. Both men drew on a hydraulic, or equilibrium, theory of physical and emotional energy. Freud seems to have come by his interest in humor because of the similarities he saw between dreams and humor. For example, he believed that each involve condensation, displacement, and transformation. Because each thinker's theories of laughter are integrated into his broader theories, it does not serve our purposes here to go into them in great depth. (For some discussions of their work, see A. Berger 1995, 121–28; P. Berger 1997, 54–56; Freud [1905] 1960, esp. chap. 6; and Morreall 1987, 99–116, 131–32). According to the relief theory of humor, emotional tension builds to deal with an upcoming social/psychological event. When the surge of energy is in excess of what is needed, the surplus is dispelled through laughter.[3]

A couple of examples might be useful to clarify this concept. Congressman Henry Hyde (R-IL) told a story involving a tense situation during the contentious 104th Congress that was defused through comic relief: "One time we were debating in the House Judiciary Committee late into the night, it was like 9:30 in the evening. We'd been at it all day—maybe twelve hours—on some issue where amendment after amendment was being offered by the Democrats and we were pretty frazzled. And all of a sudden the doors opened on the Committee and three kids come in with twenty-five pizzas and that broke up the meeting. Let me tell you, we all ended up with tomato paste on—and laughing and enjoying the evening that was pretty tense" (1998, personal interview). The pizzas had been quietly ordered by a freshman member of the committee, Sonny Bono, a professional comedian turned congressman who knew something about staging off-the-wall situations and about the comedic relief that it can create.

Another instance of comic relief took place when President George Bush was on a state visit to Japan. During a formal dinner, the president became ill, vomited on Japanese prime minister Kiichi Miyazawa, and briefly fainted. "Immediately after the president was helped from the room, Barbara Bush stood and made an accusation. She said that the incident was the fault of Emperor Akihito and Crown Prince Naruhito because they had beaten George in tennis that afternoon, 'and we Bushes aren't used to losing.' . . . When Mrs. Bush first made the accusation, the audience notably stiffened. However, as they realized she was making a joke, relief washed over the room and both Japanese and Americans burst out laughing" (Nilsen and Nilsen 2000, 234).

These three kinds of humor—superiority, incongruity, and relief humor—are included in traditional discussions of the topic. However, given our perspective of humor as social action, this typology is not complete. Not only do the winners—the top dogs—need social space for self-expression and identification, but so do the losers—those who are down-and-out in society's rankings. They need a framework to attach meaning to the world and to establish their place in it. They also need to be able to express who they are, to benefit from group solidarity, and to define individual and group values and boundaries. We can call this kind of humor *vulnerability humor,* as those who utilize it are likely to operate from a position of weakness relative to their target. Their position is a significant aspect of their humor. If they are found to have made up a story at the expense of their employer, for example, there could be employment-related penalties. Thus, if laughing equals winning and if undisguised one-upsmanship is characteristic of superiority humor, then in vulnerability humor people attempt to cover their tracks to maintain their anonymity and avoid reprisals. Among those who might be expected to use vulnerability humor are employees, relative to employers and supervisors; the physically weak, relative to those who are strong; the poor, relative to the rich; the enlisted military personnel, relative to their officers; and those who are oppressed, relative to their oppressors. Rather than confront their targets face-to-face with their humor, they discreetly tell their stories to third parties or scribble their thoughts in organizational bathrooms or elsewhere. Figuratively speaking, these people are the graffiti artists of the world.

The literature of humor identifies some types of vulnerability humor. *Gallows humor,* which was originally associated literally with the gallows, has received a fair amount of attention. A couple of jokes appear in Freud's work in which the good doctor refers to them specifically by the term gallows humor. In one case, a prisoner who is being led to his execution on a Monday comments, "Well, this week is off to a fine start!" In another, a prisoner who is about to be hanged for his offenses asks for a scarf so that he won't catch cold ([1905] 1960, 229).

During World War II sociologist Antonin Obrdlik published an article about his experiences in occupied Czechoslovakia and about the role humor played there. He expanded the concept of gallows humor from humor that applies specifically to those awaiting the gallows to persons who faced "precarious or dangerous" situations as a result of living in occupied countries: "People who live in absolute uncertainty as to their lives and property find a refuge in inventing, repeating, and spreading through the channels of whispering counterpropaganda, anecdotes and jokes about their oppressors. This is gallows humor at its best because it originates and functions among people who literally face death at any moment" (1942, 712). Similarly, Kathleen Stokker finds that humor played a very important role in developing the Norwegian resistance to Nazi occupation, even though those who created it and passed it on risked physical harm or perhaps imprisonment. Such humor counteracted Nazi propaganda; undercut the regime of Vidkun Quisling, a domestic Nazi instated by the Germans; and gave members of the general population an alternative framework with which to interpret events just after the Nazi occupation. The meaning of events of the early days of the occupation was otherwise confusing. Correspondence to Stokker, from a leader of the military branch's organized resistance, speaks of the role of gallows humor in Norway during the occupation: "I have always felt that it was a positive attitude and humor—often in the form of gallows humor—that kept us going, and helped us to see that life wasn't utterly hopeless, or at least made us refuse to admit that it was, for *that* would have meant certain defeat" (1995, 209, emphasis in original). An example of gallows humor during the occupation might be instructive: "Suspected of muttering anti-German thoughts to himself as he walked along the street, a man was brought in for questioning by the Gestapo. 'I am out of work,' he explained, 'and I was telling myself that I'd rather work for ten thousand Germans than for one Englishman.' So pleased were the Germans by this reply that they offered to help him find a job. What was his trade? 'Oh,' he answered, 'I'm a grave-digger'" (Stokker 1995, 34–35, citing Olav and Myklebust 1942).

Trickster humor is another kind discussed in the literature that can be a type of vulnerability humor. Nilsen and Nilsen, for example, discuss trickster humor as a long-standing traditional form among Native American peoples, extant before the coming of Europeans. Though they had human characteristics, these tricksters were often animals (2000, 30). Furthermore, Henry Louis Gates Jr. traces trickster humor among blacks to the continent of Africa and the African god Esu Elegbara. He argues that this type of humor arrived in America aboard the slaves ships and that it survived in the new world in a modified form as a part of African Americans' struggle to come to grips with their new circumstances (Gates 1988, esp. chaps. 1 and 2; see also, Cowan 2001, 1–24, esp. 11–12). For them trickster stories were about small, crafty animals, such as the signifying monkey or Brer Rabbit, who regularly outsmarted bigger and stronger animals of the forest, such as Brer Fox, the lion, the elephant, the alligator, and so on. Later stories were about slaves who were able to outsmart their masters (Levine 1977, 102–33, 370–86). Levine concludes that trickster stories had important social functions for blacks: "They encouraged trickery and guile; they stimulated the search for ways out of the system; they inbred a contempt for the powerful and an admiration for the perseverance and even the wisdom of the undermen; they constituted an intragroup lore which must have intensified feelings of distance from the world of the slaveholder" (132–33).

Though this type of humor is especially identified with African Americans during the time of slavery, it has wider applicability to any population that meets our definition of vulnerable. It is characterized by the extensive use of homonyms, irony, and ambiguity; as well as the mischievous use of soundalike words, double entendres, opportunistic misinterpretations of commands, and word play. Sometimes the trickster engages in deception or even outright lying. In this type of humor, members of the vulnerable population might give the appearance of acquiescing to the superior's wishes and to the superior's perceptions of what the subordinate should be; but the subordinates often mask the truth, profoundly disagreeing with their superiors. In trickster stories, the lowly trickster typically outsmarts the superior, who, although portrayed as being more powerful and more socially influential, is but slow of mind.

HUMOR AND CHANGE

Is humor liberal or conservative? Opinions vary greatly. Chris Powell, for instance, takes the position that humor is always the tool of elites who benefit from the status quo: "Differentials of power may impel subordinates to go along with a joke even when they understand but disagree with its direction, especially when directed at themselves! Invariably what is reinforced through this form of humour, and rarely challenged, is a dominant ideological position. One could go further and assert that, in any society, humour is a control resource operating both in formal and informal contexts to the advantage of powerful groups and role-players" (1988, 100). To his way of thinking, the powerless are given little choice but to submit to the control-oriented humor of elites, because the powerful determine how language will be interpreted and because attempts at humor by the powerless will be reinterpreted by elites as insolence: "Thus, for the powerless, humour, as with everything else, constitutes generally hostile terrain" (103).

Ronald Webb takes the position that most humor is conservative. He writes, "The history of humorous artifacts—jokes, stories, broadsheets, films, etc.—which come from societies which have existed in all parts of the world, strongly suggests that conservative humor has been the most prevalent type. Humor is used primarily to conserve norms and correct deviance" (1981, 41). However, he goes on to argue that another use of humor is to bring about change in society, and he identifies three ways by which this is accomplished: by degrading symbols considered sacred by dominant interests, by educating change agents to operate in an environment of change in which no one can retreat to the protection of established societal norms, and by treating all targeted institutions as if their political aspects were their most important attributes (40–47).

Historian Charles Schutz sees matters differently. He puts forth the viewpoint that, in America, humor is antiauthoritarian in nature: "A democratic political regime establishes a popularly based and politically accountable system of government pledged to the common welfare. Yet, at least in the United States, the people are profoundly anti-political and anti-government. Their negative humor strikingly corroborates a dislike and distrust evident throughout American history and politics" (1977a, 326). Schutz argues that political humor is largely obscene and this also has an antiauthoritarian consequence because it unmasks elites and subsequently performs a leveling function. At base, elites have the same biology as the rest of us, no matter their social pretensions, and in this way all people are all equal (1977b, 67; see also, Schutz 1977a, 44–45).

Discussions of humor in authoritarian systems universally hold that the leaders in such regimes do their best to ferret out humor because humor poses danger for their longevity (see, for example, Combs and Nimo 1996, 65). Arthur Asa Berger writes that humor "is used as a means of resistance by those living under authoritarian regimes and, at the same time, unites people against the governing power structure and gives them a common sense of identity" (1996, 27; see also, Stokker 1995). In an article written in the *Saturday Review* during the depths of the Cold War, Richard Hanser writes that "the commissars, like the *Gauleiter* before them, are content to be hated, but they are terrified of laughter, for no one who laughs at them can be wholly deceived, wholly subdued" (Hanser 1952, 51).

HUMOR AND POLITICAL PLURALISM

A recurring theme in humor literature is that one of the mainsprings of humor is the discrepancy between reality and what we desire and expect. To cite but one example, Roy Eckardt identifies what he calls ten "proto-jokes" about the human condition. One is the discrepancy between the "is" and the "ought": "the eternal incongruity between the world and people as they are, and world and people as they could or may become" (1992, 2; see also A. Berger 1995, 105; and P. Berger 1997, 34). Political pluralism—which encourages competition between groups who have different visions of nirvana, which has a system of checks and balances between multiple branches of government, and which demonstrates its need for continuous compromise—creates circumstances in which there is and always will be a discrepancy between what is desired and reality. And the strained compromises of political actors appear foolish when compared to the obvious simplicity of common sense, echoes of the saying that a camel is a horse designed by a committee.

For Charles Schutz, the end of pluralistic politics could never be some high, moralistic state, because that would be the end of politics itself: "Politics can not be a drama for the staging of high moral actions and great decisions of earth-shaking consequences. We may seek to project the appearance of such and play to its roles, but the political drama founded on a pluralistic society burlesques us. The Alphonse of our revealed truth collides with the Gaston of another's vision of truth, and the pratfall of compromise results" (1977a, 322–23; see also, 308). Still, for Schutz, humor brings real benefits to the political system. A main theme he develops is that humor is aggression through words; but, when converted to humor, aggressiveness loses much of its edge (309). Further, once participants can subject to humor those ideas they hold close, they become more prepared to compromise (330–31). And because humor brings a disposition toward compromise, it steers the regime away from the extremes of the Right and the Left (299).

Combs and Nimmo also discuss the comic aspects of political pluralism, but the writers are not so sanguine about their consequences. They see futility rather than functionality. Because nothing can be accomplished in Congress because of its many factions blocking each other, it does nothing: "The comedy in the congressional situation is that members have achieved a state of group relations that makes it imperative that nothing happen, so that they may all coexist together in a perfect world of inactivity. Better rituals of execration followed by reconciliation than pragmatic activity that threatens the internal bliss and continuity of the group" (1996, 138). Similarly, according to Combs and Nimmo, modern presidents are much less than we expect them to be. As mediated by the post-Watergate press, presidents are presented as fools, not as lionhearted figures suitable to wear the mantle of Washington, Lincoln, or either of the Roosevelts: "*Rather than a heroic, or a tragic figure, the president has been transformed into a comic figure.* The press once enhanced the popular view of the president as a heroic figure until proven otherwise; now the story line is that the president is hapless, inadequate, incompetent, and a bungler" (110, emphasis in text). And so it is, the authors contend, with the other political institutions—the courts, the parties, the bureaucracy—all of whom are caught in the tragic–comic chasm between intention and reality, and all subject to humor because the democratic myth is too precious to let go and because the reality is comic when compared to the myth.

ORGANIZATION

In chapter 2, we look at congressional humor over the years, utilizing (among other sources) biographies of House and Senate members who are noted for their humor. We let them tell us about congressional humor, its characteristics, and how it was regarded by members over the years. In chapter 3 we examine humorous stories handed down and retold in the U.S. Senate to find out what they might tell us about Senate norms. These stories are clever and humorous, but they also often contain scripts about what kinds of behavior are acceptable and what kind are not. Chapters 4 and 5 respectively look at the integration of African Americans and women into the institution of Congress. We see that humor plays an important role in the integration of each group, but functions in a very different way in the case of women and African Americans. Each had its own history, so each had to adopt strategies for inclusion based on an assessment of what was possible and likely to bring success. Finally, chapter 6 draws on interviews with current and recent members of Congress, who discuss such matters as the advantages and dangers of humor, the ways they create humor, and their views about the humor of other members of Congress. Throughout, this book illustrates how humor has played an important role in the institution of Congress, though it also demonstrates that what has been considered acceptable humor has changed over time, thereby reflecting changes in society. Altogether, a reasonable concern with humor sheds insights about how Congress socializes new members, how it integrates new elements into its membership, how it seeks to keep conflict within bounds, and how it facilitates change.

NOTES

1. A problem for the superiority theorists of humor is that they do not provide the tools to distinguish between superiority humor and wanton cruelty. The latter may contain many of the elements of the former. Its purpose may be to demonstrate the superiority of the perpetrator over the victim; there may be surprise when the perpetrator suddenly reveals his or her intentions; and there may be laughter, maybe even guttural laughter, on the part of the perpetrator, resulting from the relief at being able to successfully carry out the heinous act.

2. Though we have classified Bergson and Koestler as incongruity theorists (as do other students of humor), their treatments of humor, as one might expect, are broad. In addition to their main emphasis on incongruity as a source of humor, they write about the importance of recognizing the role of aggression in humor. For instance, Bergson writes, "laughter is really and truly a kind of social 'ragging'" and "In laughter, we always find an unavowed intention to humiliate, and consequently to correct our neighbour, if not in his will, at least in his deed" ([1900] 1956, 148). Similarly, Koestler writes, "However much the opinions of the theorists differ, on this one point nearly all of them agree: that the emotions discharged in laughter always contain an element of aggressiveness" (1997, 683).

3. What was said about Bergson and Koestler in the previous note is true of Freud as well. Though we present his unique contribution as that of a relief-humor theorist (as do others), he also saw humor as aggressive. Thus, he writes that "the purposes of jokes can easily be reviewed. Where a joke is not an aim in itself—that is, where it is not an innocent one—there are only two purposes that it may serve, and these two can themselves be subsumed under a single heading. It is either a *hostile* joke (serving the purpose of aggressiveness, satire, or defence) or an *obscene* joke (serving the purpose of exposure)" ([1905] 1960, 96–97, emphasis in original). And Koestler, though he is treated as an incongruity theorist, nonetheless discusses the emotional relief that results in the course of humor, for example, when he writes, "The emotion discharged in course laughter is aggression robbed of its purpose" Koestler 1997, 683).

Finally, it must be noted that a single joke may have elements of both superiority and incongruity humor. As well, depending on the perceptions of audiences, a single joke could have elements of all three—superiority, incongruity, and relief humor.

2

Congressional Humor, from John Randolph of Roanoke to Mo Udall

I wouldn't giv two cents to be a Congresser. The wus insult I ever received was when sertin citizens of Baldinsville axed me to run fur the Legislater. Sez I, "My frends, dostest think I'd stoop to that there?" . . . I spoke in my most orfullest tones, & they knowed I wasn't to be trifled with.

—Artemus Ward

There is a congressional humor lore that consists of humorous stories, exchanges, and incidents that get passed on—told and retold and embellished—over several decades or more within the institution of Congress. This lore is found in stories that members tell one another; in the autobiographies of congressional members who are noted for their humor; and in the writings of other members who, though not particularly gifted with humor themselves, nonetheless appreciate good stories and include them in their books. When occasionally humorous stories cease to be passed on, historians of congressional humor may find such stories during research and in this way preserve them as part of the lore of congressional humor. Another source of congressional humor that contributes to the preservation of lore is the occasional book of jokes and stories about humorous incidents occurring in Congress, usually during a specific period.

In this chapter, we look at congressional humor over time, especially drawing on the perceptions of House and Senate members who over the years have been recognized as gifted humorists or students of congressional humor and who have written chapters or even entire books on the subject. These congressional humorists include Samuel "Sunset" Cox, James Beauchamp "Champ" Clark, James E. Watson, Alben W. Barkley, Sam J. Ervin, Jr., Alexander Wiley, Brooks Hays, and Morris K. Udall. All together, their years in Congress span the period from 1857 until 1989, and their humor and writings contribute mightily to the lore of congressional humor.[1] It is doubtful that any of these men, save possibly for Samuel Cox, systematically studied the writings of the philosophers, social scientists, or other scholars on the topic of humor for the specific purpose of improving their practical humor skills. They didn't have to; they came by it naturally. The world of the congressperson is a fast-moving world in which members have to be able to intuit proper responses with lightening speed, yet they have to do so within the parameters of such constraints as the culture of the time, the norms of the institution, the role they choose to play within Congress, and the nature of the specific interaction.

CONGRESSIONAL HUMOR AT THE CREATION

The Congress newly created under the Constitution of 1789 had the barest outlines of structure provided for it in the document itself, but these were soon to be supplemented by formal rules adopted by each house. The other guiding principles so important to getting things done, such as the informal rules and expectations, would have to be worked out over decades of interactions. Thus, we can expect humor, with its playful but risky character—and its ambiguity—in these early years, for most members would be tentative, cautious, and exploratory as they sought to find their way in the thicket of expectations of a new institution. Without rules and norms, it would be too easy to be misunderstood. For a few, such as those who were unconcerned with the developing norms of the institution or with being integrated into them, we might expect the humor to be raucous, outrageous, and even intensely personal. The looseness of control in the early times would allow a wide berth for such individual behavior. What is handed down from the early years in the congressional humor lore is mostly of the latter kind, and much of that involves the acerbic and abrasively personal comic invective of John Randolph of Roanoke, a Jeffersonian Republican from Virginia (and, likewise, humor of the same nature but with Randolph as the target of others).

Randolph has been described as a beardless bachelor with an unusually shrill voice. It was rumored during his life and confirmed after his death that he was impotent, and speculation had it that this may have been the source of much of his bitterness (Harris 1964, 53). A cousin of Thomas Jefferson, Randolph was an aristocrat who had an eccentric character and who dressed and appeared accordingly.

Another notable figure is Samuel "Sunset" Cox, who is an indispensable link to early congressional humor. Because his first term in Congress slightly preceded the Civil War, he was able to acquire first- and second-hand information about the masters of humor in the early Congresses. And he did. Spurred by his deep interest in congressional humor, he not only sought out those who served before him for their recollections of humor in Congress, but he was also an astute observer of humor in Congress during the years that he served. About Randolph, Cox quotes a contemporary: "His person was as unique as his manner. He was tall and extremely slender. His habit was to wear an overcoat extending to the floor, with an upright standing collar, which concealed his entire person except his head, which seemed to be set by the ears upon the collar of his coat. . . . His face was wan, wrinkled, and without beard; his limbs long and unsightly, especially his arms and fingers; his skin seemed to grow to the attenuated bone, and the large, ill-formed joints were extremely ugly. But those fingers, and especially the right forefinger, gave point and *vim* to his wit and invective" ([1880] 1969, 149–50, emphasis in the text).

Randolph had a quick wit, which was used to cut down other members. While speaking to the Missouri Compromise of 1820, when he paused to collect his thoughts, he was interrupted several times by Philomen Beecher of Ohio, with a motion to move the previous question. After a number of such interruptions, Randolph finally commented, "Mr. Speaker, in the Netherlands, a man of small capacity, with bits of wood and leather, will, in a few moments, construct a toy that, with the pressure of the finger and thumb, will cry 'Cuckoo! cuckoo!' With less ingenuity, and with inferior materials, the people of Ohio have made a toy that will, without much pressure, cry, 'Previous question, Mr. Speaker! previous question, Mr. Speaker!' at the same time pointing at his victim with his skeleton finger. The House was convulsed" (Cox [1880] 1969, 150).

John Randolph at times received as well as he gave, but he was seldom without a retort. One such sizzling personal exchange took place between him and Congressman Tristam Burges, a former humanities professor, in which Burges brought up Randolph's rumored impotence:

BURGES: Sir, Divine Providence takes care of his own universe. Moral monsters cannot propagate. Impotent of everything except malevolence of purpose, they can not otherwise multiply miseries than by blaspheming all that is pure and prosperous and happy. Could demon propagate demon, the universe might become a pandemonium; but I rejoice that the Father of Lies can never become the Father of Liars. One adversary of God and man is enough for one universe.

RANDOLPH: You pride yourself on an animal faculty, in respect to which the slave is your equal and the jackass infinitely your superior. (Harris 1964, 54)

He prided himself in his opposition to the presidencies of John Adams and John Quincy Adams: "I bore some humble part in putting down the dynasty of John the First, and by the grace of God, I hope to aid in putting down the dynasty of John the Second" (Harris 1964, 56). John Quincy Adams returned the sentiment when he characterized Randolph thus:

> His face is ashen, gaunt his whole body,
> His breath is green with gall; his tongue drips poison. (Harris 1964, 56)

Randolph reacted to Richard Rush's selection as secretary of the treasury by commenting, "Never were abilities so much below mediocrity so well rewarded; no, not when Caligula's horse was made consul" (Harris 1964, 53). When President Andrew Jackson nominated Edward Livingston to be secretary of state, Randolph spewed, "He is a man of splendid abilities, but utterly corrupt. He shines and stinks like rotten mackerel by moonlight. . . . Of Congressional colleagues, Robert Wright and John Rae he said that the House exhibited two anomalies, 'A Wright always wrong; and a Rae without light'" (Boller 1991, 184). When another colleague, Samuel Dexter, changed his position on an issue before Congress, Randolph called him "Mr. Ambi-Dexter" (Boller 1991, 184).

The relationship between Randolph and Henry Clay figures in the congressional humor literature. According to one story, when the two once met on a narrow sidewalk, Clay proudly proclaimed, "I, Sir, do not step aside for a scoundrel," to which Randolph, stepping out of the way and waving Clay on, replied, "On the other hand, I always do!" (Harris 1964, 62–63; Harris notes correctly that the order in some versions of this story is reversed, with Clay waving Randolph by). Clay was a perennial candidate for the White House, a situation about which Randolph is alleged to have commented, "Clay's eye is on the presidency; and my eye is on him" (Harris 1964, 61).

However, Randolph's time in the Congress was also one in which real and perceived slights among gentlemen were settled by duels. *Code duello* was imported into this country during the time of the American Revolution by officers of European nations who came to fight in the Revolutionary War, especially those from France, and it continued into the Civil War (Boller 1991, 38–41). A person could be challenged to a duel for inadvertent behavior and for remarks that were simply misinterpreted. Randolph's slashing invective made him a strong candidate to be so challenged, sooner or later. It came to pass when he spoke disparagingly of Clay in a speech made in Congress on March 30, 1826. Clay's shift of support to John Quincy Adams in the disputed election of 1824 had caused him to be the brunt of many caustic remarks about a foul bargain between him and Adams that resulted in the Kentuckian being appointed secretary of state in the Adams administration. Randolph, who had been among the most strident critics of Clay, "compared Adams and Clay to two unsavory characters in Henry Fielding's popular novel, *Tom Jones*: 'the coalition of Blifil and Black George . . . the combination unheard of till then of the Puritan and the blackleg.'" Clay resented being referred to as a "blackleg," or crooked gambler, and the challenge ensued (Boller 1991, 37–38).

The two met on April 8, 1826, on the Virginia side of the Potomac, accompanied by their seconds, a surgeon, and their mutual friend Senator Thomas Hart Benton (D-MO). When Randolph's pistol misfired, Clay gave him another chance. On the first round, each missed the other. Benton stepped in to stop the duel at that point, but both men insisted that it go on. In the second exchange, the bullet from Clay's pistol passed through Randolph's cape while Randolph deliberately fired his shot into the air, then ran over to Clay to shake his hand. Pointing to the hole in his cape he announced, "You owe me a new coat, Mr. Clay," to which Clay answered, "I am glad the debt is not greater." It was later revealed that the evening before Randolph had told a friend, "I have determined to receive without returning Clay's fire; nothing shall induce me to harm a hair on his head. I will not make his wife a widow, or his children orphans. Their tears would be shed over his grave, but when the sod of Virginia rests on my bosom there is not in this wide world one individual to pay his tribute upon me" (for accounts of this famous duel, see Boller 1991, 38; Harris 1964, 63).

Dueling notwithstanding, Cox made the point that true wit is spontaneous and does not have the malice of forethought: "In my talk with Mr. Burgess [*sic*] he spoke kindly of all his early competitors; and Randolph, when dying, was called on by his old antagonist, Clay. It was the grasped hand, the knightly honor, and the tender tear—these show the springs of sensibility, the secret of rhetorical power" ([1880] 1969, 152).

The acutely sarcastic and personal humor of Randolph did not become a norm for the new Congress. This is not to say that members in years to come did not engage in sarcasm or make light of the mannerisms or personal characteristics of fellow congressmen. As Cox put it, "The most weighty, or, rather, the best, speech is listened to with fatigue unless there be an occasional smart *double entendre*, tart retort, tickling piquancy, personal point, or pertinent fact. That which draws most, which empties the members' seats to fill the area in front of the Speaker's desk, is the bellicose" ([1880] 1969, 185 [emphasis in original]). Rather, it is to suggest that within the first few decades of the creation of Congress, a type of humor developed that was playful and that drew on the clever usage of language, ironies, and discontinuities of thought. This is consistent with the creation of social norms to foster civil relationships in the new legislative institution. The development of a more gentle humor would, of course, also serve as a lubricant to facilitate the work of that body.

Cox mentions several members of Congress who served during the first half of the nineteenth century who were skilled in the use of this playful humor, which, incidentally, Cox personally preferred. He especially singles out Benjamin "Meat Axe" Hardin (W-KY), Thomas Corwin (W-R-OH) and Henry Clay (W-KY). It is interesting to note the characteristics that Cox draws on to describe their humor. He writes that Tom Corwin once told him that "Hardin was the most entertaining man he ever knew" ([1880] 1969, 195). Cox acknowledges that Hardin, who served in the House intermittently between 1815 and 1837, was known by the sobriquet "Meat Axe" and that Randolph said of him that he was "a butcher-knife sharpened on a brick-bat" ([1880] 1969, 196). But Cox disagrees with this characterization: "He was rather of the humorous than of the witty kind. The butcher-knife is too course and the vendetta dirk too polished to describe his quality" ([1880] 1969, 197). Since most of Hardin's humor was spontaneous, not much of it has survived. One story about him, perhaps apocryphal, has him on his death bed. In his last hours, he sent for several preachers. "One of them said to him, 'You have had a Catholic priest; you've had a Presbyterian minister; you've had a Methodist parson; I am a Campbellite. What do you mean by it?' 'Well,' replied Hardin, 'Mr. Preacher, I am on my last legs and about to go, they tell me. I've heard that heaven is a very good place to go, and I want to take all the chances of getting there'" (Boykin 1961, 401).

In discussing the humor of Henry Clay (W-KY), a towering political presence for most of the first half of the nineteenth century, Cox once again emphasizes the beneficial qualities of his humor—his playfulness as well as his sense of boundaries: "He was at times playful as a colt with his fancies, but he always had them under curb. . . . His mirth constantly restored and preserved the good temper of the Senate" ([1880] 1969, 134). James Buchanan was a special target for his "stingless fun." Buchanan

was somewhat cross-eyed, and had little specific levity. Mr. Clay was referring to the Democratic leaders, at the same time looking at Silas Wright, between whom and himself sat Mr. Buchanan. Mr. Buchanan rose and said "he was sorry the Senator from Kentucky was so often disposed to pay his respects to him." "But," said Mr. Clay, "I had no allusion to you when I spoke of the *leaders*, but to another Senator," pointing to Silas Wright.

MR. BUCHANAN: The Senator looked at me when he spoke.

MR. CLAY: No, Mr. President, I did not look at him.

And then, holding up and crossing his two forefingers with the mischievous air of a Puck, and his eye all twinkling with fun, he said, "It was the way *he* looked at *me*!" The laugh went round heartily. ([1880] 1969, 134–35, emphasis in original)

In another instance, when Buchanan was defending himself against charges of disloyalty during the War of 1812, he pointed out that he joined a company of volunteers at the time of the battle of North Point and marched into Baltimore, albeit after the British had retreated, to which Clay inquired, "Will you be good enough to inform us whether the British retreated in consequence of your valiantly marching to the relief of Baltimore, or whether you marched to the relief of Baltimore in consequence of the British having already retreated" ([1880] 1969, 135–36)?

A third member of Congress whom Cox singles out for his use of extravagant humor is Thomas Corwin (W-R-OH), who served during the first half of the nineteenth century in both the House and the Senate (intermittently between 1831 and 1861) and who was nicknamed "Black Tom" because of his swarthy complexion. In discussing Corwin's humor, Cox describes the skills Corwin brought to the art, which draw on playfulness, sometimes including the use of satire, but satire that was lighthearted, not mean: "In all the elements, from the lowest burlesque to the finest wit, Thomas Corwin was confessedly the master. He drew from the arsenal all the weapons of parliamentary warfare; but how seldom he used them! His effusions were brilliant, fervid, eloquent, pathetic, but, above all, his satire, while keen, was not poisoned or barbed with ill-temper. It was pertinent and powerful, demolishing, yet stingless" ([1880] 1969, 200).

Much of Corwin's humor came from his timing, gestures, variation in tone, and facial expressions. Thus, Cox writes of him, "He is best remembered for lighter efforts, as when he started in full opulence of illustration after the foible of a fellow member. No one, unless he has seen his facial expression and heard his variety of tone, can imagine his power" ([1880] 1969, 200–201). One of his most famous House performances came on February 15, 1840, when Corwin satirized General Crary (D-MI) at great length in response to Crary's critical speech regarding William Henry Harrison's lack of strategy at the battle of Tippecanoe. His speech was so devastating that a few days later ex-president John Quincy Adams, then a member of the House, referred to Crary as "the late General Crary of Michigan," and the label stuck. Decades later, when Champ Clark (D-MO) read the text of this speech in its original, he was disappointed, given its legendary status in congressional humor lore, and he commented to another member, General Grosvenor (R-OH), that either the text he read was incomplete or Corwin was overrated as a humorist. "Neither proposition is true," replied the general. "Tom Corwin was not overrated, but no report of his humorous speeches, however accurate, will sustain his reputation. His wonderful effect upon an audience depended more on his marvelous facial expression than upon anything he said" (Clark 1920, 206). Grosvenor went on to tell about an incident in which Corwin got into a heated exchange with a high-spirited hometown preacher. Everyone expected that the preacher would eviscerate Corwin from the pulpit

the following Sunday, and each attended the service "to enjoy the skinning." Corwin himself took a seat in the "amen corner," facing the con-
gregation but out of sight of the preacher.

> The preacher did not know Corwin was in the audience, but he proceeded to
> excoriate him nevertheless. As the preacher spoke, Corwin, facing the audi-
> ence, punctuated and illustrated the speech with all sorts of facial contortions
> and grimaces. Interrogation points, exclamation points, and all sorts of
> points and comments appeared upon Tom's dark and mobile countenance.
> The audience began to smile, the smiles grew into titters, and at some severe
> thrust made by the preacher, and some extraordinary facial grimace by Cor-
> win, the audience burst into a roar of laughter. The preacher looked around,
> saw Corwin, and grew so angry that he quit speaking suddenly, and left the
> victory to Corwin. (Clark 1920, 207)

ADVANTAGES OF HUMOR

These skilled users of humor who have been members of Congress over
the years were thoughtful people, and, quite naturally, they have reflected
on the nature of humor, its advantages and its dangers. They conceived of
humor as a gift—a talent they possessed that was not shared by most others. Skilled congressional humorists believed that humor was beneficial to
them in their work as legislators and that it made important contributions
to the work of a legislature. They agreed that members who disparage humor probably did not have a sense of it. Being skilled with humor, they
also considered its downsides—that is, the kind of humor likely to get
them into trouble and the importance of time and place. As thoughtful
people, albeit risk takers, they knew that every attempt at humor was a
calculated prediction about outcomes.

That early student of humor Congressman Cox writes that skill in using humor is one of the greatest gifts a politician could possess: "No one,
except the most jaundiced, but will confess that the talent for wit or humor is one of the most potential in influencing men, and especially bodies of men. If administration or legislation consists in understanding how
to thread the avenues to the heart, if to please is to rule, who will account
such a gift useless in human society? Those who most depreciate the talent are those who are void of it" ([1880] 1969, 123).

Champ Clark, longtime Speaker of the House and a leading contender
for the Democratic nomination for president in 1912, writes about the advantages of humor: "Wit and humor, like all the other numberless and
precious gifts of God to man, undoubtedly have their proper uses. They
help to float a heavy speech, and they give wings to solid arguments. A
brilliant sally, a sparkling epigram, a 'fetching sim-i-le, a happy mot, an

apropos anecdote, may extricate one from an embarrassing predicament where all else would utterly fail" (1920, 186). Six decades later, Senator Sam Ervin Jr. (D-NC) expressed similar sentiments when he wrote, "As a trial lawyer, politician, and legislator, I recognize the pragmatic value of humor. An ounce of revealing humor often has more power to reveal, convince, or ridicule than do many tons of erudite argument" (1983, 5).

One noted humorist in Congress finds that among the advantages of humor is that it reduces tension and lends cohesion and healing to the rough and tumble of politics. "Politics is one of the greatest sources of tensions," writes Brooks Hays (D-AR), who served eight terms in the House, from 1943 to 1959. "Humor can become a cohesive force, and laughter a healing exercise; and in this decade of civil strife and serious problems beyond the seas, when frustration engenders bitterness and passions arise, this precious quality of humor may be our saving grace. It may strengthen our faith and enable us to enjoy companionship, even with those who are on opposing sides" (1968, 3).

A member of the House from 1961 to 1991, Morris Udall (D-AZ) also stresses the palliative benefits of humor: "Political humor leavens the public dialogue; it invigorates the body politic; it uplifts the national spirit. . . . In times of national tragedy, disappointment or defeat, political humor can assuage the nation's grief, sadness, or anger and thus make bearable that which must be borne. . . . Humor is also the best antidote for the politician's occupational disease: an inflated, overweening, suffocating sense of self-importance. . . . Politics is a people business—and people crave laughter" (1988, xiii–xiv). Alben Barkley (D-KY), who was known for his storytelling, agrees that humor helped him keep his perspective while in public life (Barkley 1954, 18–20).

Congressional humorists believe that one type of humor, self-effacing humor, is a shoo-in for striking a resonate cord with the audience. Having lost his vision in a childhood accident, Representative Udall had his "one-eyed jokes" always at the ready: "Sammy Davis, the famous entertainer, lost an eye in an accident and converted to Judaism. One time he went golfing, and someone asked him, 'Sammy, what is your handicap?' Sammy said, 'Handicap? Man, I'm a one-eyed Negro Jew, do I need one?' During my presidential campaign, I would add, 'Handicap? I'm a one-eyed Mormon Democrat from conservative Arizona. . . . You can't find a higher handicap than that" (1988, 92). Representative Brooks Hays did not like to run the risk of humor that might hurt others, but he commented, "A joke told by the speaker on himself, is quite a different matter, and never fails to receive an appreciative response" (1968, 5).

The recounting of humorous stories from the past contributes to the cohesion of an organization and to its shared meanings. To be a witness to one of these playful events is something to be treasured, so members wait on the speeches of fellow members who are known for their humor and gladly recount such experiences to the less fortunate.

Certainly one of the more hair-raising of shared congressional experiences is the maiden speech. When one rises and asks for the Speaker's attention to make one's first utterance from the floor, the timing must be right, the message must be weighty, and the emotion must be controlled. Of maiden speeches, it is doubtful that any were any more playful than that by "Private" John Allen (D-MS), who served from 1885 to 1901. Champ Clark recalls this event:

> The River and Harbor bill was up. John wanted to offer an amendment making an appropriation for the Tombigbee River. The chairman of the committee, Mr. Willis of Kentucky, had promised him time, and had then forgotten it. John asked unanimous consent to address the House, and Willis tried to help him get it; but some one objected, whereupon John, with tears in his voice and looking doleful as a hired mourner at a funeral, said, with melancholy accent:
>
> "Well, I would at least like to have permission to print some remarks in *The Record*, and insert 'laughter and applause' in appropriate places." That was his astonishing exordium. The palpable hit at one of the most common abuses of the House—"leave to print"—tickled the members greatly, and he secured the unanimous consent which he desired. He closed that speech with an amazing exhibition of assurance, which added to his fame more than the speech itself. He wound up by saying, "Now Mr. Speaker, having fully answered all the arguments of my opponents, I will retire to the cloak-room for a few moments, to receive the congratulations of admiring friends"—which set the galleries wild with delight. (Clark 1920, 200–201)

A very different experience, though nonetheless playful, is the maiden speech of the ever dour, ever frugal H. R. Gross (R-IA). A freshman member of the House in 1949, he was anxious about when and how he would make his first speech, and he raised this concern with veteran member Clare Hoffman (R-MI), who responded, "Nothing to it. I'm making a long speech tomorrow, and somewhere you stop me and ask a question. I'll answer it, and that will take care of your first speech." The two rehearsed exactly how and when this was to take place, along with the question to be asked. The next day, Hoffman made his speech as scheduled, and at the agreed-on time, Gross rose to ask if the congressman would yield the floor for a question. Hoffman courteously yielded, and Gross asked the scripted question and then sat down to receive the reply. "Hoffman's reply fixed the moment indelibly in Gross's memory. 'I cannot understand,' said Hoffman, 'what possessed the gentleman from Iowa to ask such a stupid question'" (O'Neal and O'Neal 1964, 110–11).

Among the skills of politicians, probably none is more important than facile use of language. Whether they attempt humor or not, congresspersons are likely to be exceptionally smooth in language usage, and they admire skillful displays by their colleagues. Members especially recount those effective speeches that use language playfully, of which one of the most frequently mentioned was the delightfully sarcastic "Duluth speech" of J. Proctor Knott (D-KY), delivered on January 27, 1871. The occasion was the request for an appropriation of public land to build a railroad from the St. Croix River to Lake Superior. Knott, in his first term, rose to speak against it and did so with such gusto that there were shouts from members asking that he be allowed to continue his impromptu performance beyond the allotted time. The speech is long, so we can only sample it to give the reader a taste of its delicious, albeit biting, humor. Knott began by stating that he had never heard of Duluth and that he had great difficulty even finding a map that showed its whereabouts.

And now, Mr. Speaker, in the middle of these teeming pine-barrens at the mouth of the St. Croix, is Duluth—Duluth, Zenith City of the Unsalted Seas. *(Laughter.)* Duluth! The word fell upon my ear with peculiar and indescribable charm, like the gentle murmur of a low fountain stealing forth in the midst of roses, or the soft, sweet accents of an angel's whisper in the bright, joyous dream of sleeping innocence. Duluth! 'Twas the name for which my soul had panted for years, as the hart panteth for the water-brooks. *(Renewed laughter.)* But where was Duluth? Never in all my limited reading had my vision been gladdened by seeing the celestial word in print. *(Laughter.)* And I felt a profounder humiliation in my ignorance that its dulcet syllables had never before ravished my delighted ears. *(Roars of laughter.)* . . . Nevertheless, I was confident that it existed somewhere, and that its discovery would constitute the crowning glory of the present century, if not of all modern times. *(Laughter.)* I knew it was bound to exist, in the very nature of things; that the symmetry and perfection of our planetary system would be incomplete without it *(renewed laughter);* that the elements of material nature would long since have resolved themselves back into original chaos if there had been such a hiatus in creation as would have resulted in leaving out Duluth. *(Roars of laughter.)* In fact, sir, I was overwhelmed with the conviction that Duluth not only existed somewhere, but that, wherever it was, it was a great and glorious place. (Boykin 1961, 272–73)

Although speech in Congress turned more bland over the next century, colleagues nonetheless turned out to hear Senator Everett McKinley Dirksen (R-IL), who served as minority leader in the Senate from 1959 to 1969. Dirksen could be counted on to plead his case year after year, with mock profundity and in the most florid language, for the merits of the marigold and why it should be our national flower: "It is as sprightly as the daffodil . . . as colorful as the rose, as resolute as the zinnia, as delicate as the chrysanthemum, as aggressive as the petunia, as ubiquitous as the violet, and as stately as the snapdragon. It beguiles the senses and ennobles the spirit of man. . . . Since it is native to America, and nowhere else in the world, and common to every state in the Union, I present the American marigold for designation as the national floral emblem of our country" (MacNeil 1970, 216). His linguistic exuberance was also in evidence once when he returned to the Senate after a short stay in the hospital, only to find that three favorite Republican bills had been narrowly defeated in his absence. He intoned, "To my bedridden amazement, my pajama-fluffed consternation, yes, to my pill-laden astonishment, I learned they were victims of that new White House telephonic half-Nelson known as the Texas Twist" (Kenworthy 1969, 4).

DANGERS OF USING HUMOR

The great nineteenth-century congressional humorist Tom Corwin of Ohio advised James Garfield to "never make the people laugh. If you would succeed in life, you must be solemn, solemn as an ass. All great monuments are built over solemn asses" (Schutz 1977a, 24). Senator James Watson writes, "Senator Tom Corwin, the matchless orator from Ohio, always believed he would have been president had it not been for his story-telling proclivities and his frequent recourse to wit in his contests on the stump" (1936, 42). More depressing yet, Cox writes, "Before [Corwin] died he told a friend that he would only be remembered after his death as a clown" ([1880] 1969, 124).

And Corwin was not alone in his apprehension about the consequences of being humorous. Just as congressional humorists sang humor's praises, they were also acutely aware of its dangers. They knew that it was always subject to misinterpretation—nigh, even to be taken as serious talk—thereby leaving them open to charges of insensitivity. The downside to which they were probably most sensitive is the risk of not being taken as serious people trying to make their points. Champ Clark wrote that the many who were not good at humor were jealous of the few who were so blessed, and he referred to them as the "dry as dusts." He wrote, "To be disparaged is the penalty which brilliancy must pay to dullness. . . . As the non-humorous and unwitty constitute the overwhelming majority, they have succeeded, partially at least, by dint of ceaseless iteration, in propagating the idea that mental dryness is indicative of wisdom and that a wit or humorist is lacking in the substantive qualities of mind—all of which is mere moonshine" (1920, 186).

Senator Sam Ervin Jr. (D-NC), who served in the Senate from 1954 to 1974, echoes many of Champ Clark's concerns: "Unfortunately, humor has always been in low repute among people whose over-serious minds ban it from their hearts. This is true nowadays of misanthropes who multiply their miseries by decrying the therapeutic potency of humor and by refusing to take dosages of it for their pessimism. They equate humor with buffoonery and allege that its devotees are silly fools unconcerned with the problems that bedevil humanity" (1983, ix). Alben Barkely sardonically advised ambitious politicians to regard themselves and everything they did "with the utmost gravity," noting that in the 1952 presidential campaign, Republicans "circulated the ugly insinuation that Adlai E. Stevenson was a congenitally witty man" (Barkley 1954, 18).

Truth be told, there is a real danger that humor might overshadow the serious message the politician is attempting to convey. While campaigning during the early 1930s with Senator Joe T. Robinson (D-AR, later Senate minority and majority leader), Brooks Hays noted that Robinson did not use anecdotes or humor in his speeches. When Hays inquired as to the reason, Robinson answered that "he had deliberately renounced using humor because he feared the audience would remember only the jokes and forget the serious content of his talks" (Hays 1968, 1–2). It seems that while unhitching his horse after a speech, Robinson heard farmers commenting about his stories: "There wasn't a word said . . . about the serious side of my speech! I decided then and there that I would drop humor, in all of its forms, from my speeches" (Hays 1968, 2).

One might be an avid admirer of humor but still not be good user of it. Senator Henry "Scoop" Jackson (D-WA) is said to be one such person. He attended a program where a story was told about Nixon's returning to the White House after the president had resigned. "Entering the Oval Office, he stumbled and bumped into President Gerry Ford. 'Oh, *pardon* me, Gerry,' Nixon said. 'I already did, Dick,' Ford replied.' The next night Jackson ventured to tell the same anecdote. Unfortunately, when he delivered the punch line he had Nixon saying, '*Excuse* me, Gerry,' and Ford replying, 'I already did, Dick.' Nobody got the joke and of course nobody laughed" (Udall 1988, 192, emphasis in the original). To attempt to share humor to nobody's delight is to face excruciating embarrassment.

RIDICULE

Ridicule is the hot poker of humor. It can be fun, it can be well received, and it can make its creator look very clever. On the flip side, it can be misunderstood, with the consequence of making its author appear mean-spirited; or, as another scenario, the instigator might be "upped" and made to look like a fool.

Though most congresspersons emphasize the positive functions of political humor, a few also mention that ridicule is an important function of humor because, if members fear they might be ridiculed, it gives the ridiculer a relative position of power over them. For instance, Senator Sam Ervin writes, "When they employ humor to achieve objectives, men do so to amuse, to reveal, to convince, to chide, *to ridicule,* or to alleviate tensions, burdens and woes" (1983, 5, emphasis added). Indeed, in defending the censure recommendation of the select committee established to investigate the abuses of Senator Joseph McCarthy, Ervin chose, as a deliberate strategy, to ridicule the infamous senator from Wisconsin because Ervin thought McCarthy would be most vulnerable to this approach. Thus, speaking on the floor in defense of the committee report, Ervin said,

> The writer of Ecclesiastes assures us that "there is nothing new under the sun." The McCarthy technique of lifting statements out of context was practiced in North Carolina about seventy-five years ago. At that time the women had a habit of wearing their hair in topknots. This preacher deplored that habit. As a consequence, he preached a rip-snorting sermon one Sunday on the text, "Top Not Come Down." At the conclusion of his sermon an irate woman, wearing a very pronounced topknot, told the preacher that no such text could be found in the Bible. The preacher thereupon opened the Scriptures to the seventeenth verse of the twenty-fourth chapter of Matthew and pointed to the words "Let him which is on the housetop not come down to take anything out of this house." Any practitioner of the McCarthy technique of lifting things out of context can readily find the text "top not come down" in this verse. (Ervin 1983, 162)

Some congresspersons who are known to be skilled at ridicule nonetheless indicate a clear preference for a softer kind of humor. Among them is our aforementioned friend Samuel Cox. In his insightful book *Why We Laugh,* he writes of humor: "Humor has no sting. It is not poisonous, like the Stygian waters, which no other vessel but a mule's hoof could hold. The humorous man is, from his very sensibility, likely to be gentle and pathetic, but not malignant. He can rain tears as well as bring smiles" ([1880] 1969, 14). He carefully distinguishes between "humor," "wit," and "farce": "Wit cuts, humor tickles, farce grins, humor smiles. . . . While wit uses the scalpel, brings blood, divides our members, cuts out the gangrene, and oftentimes the healthy parts, humor manipulates gently, or gestures with the playful finger under the ribs of jollity, never drawing blood, but pumping up the moisture until our eyes run over with gladness. . . . Wit is not always a desirable quality. The worst men often use it. The devil generally monopolizes it" (16). According to Cox, humor is spontaneous and depends on a basic human goodness: "The observation of the writer is that the best humor is that which springs out of its surroundings. No jest depending merely on memory strikes kindly, strikes home, or strikes hard. Besides, studied invective implies malice aforethought, and no malicious man was great either in wit or humor" (151).

Still, few who have ever served in Congress could match "Sunset" Cox
for his quick and cutting retorts. In a debate over a Rivers and Harbors
Bill in 1880, the rotund representative from Michigan Roswell G. Horr,
who tipped the scale at 250 pounds, made the near-fatal mistake of referring to Cox as "my genial little friend." Cox, who was quite conscious of
his diminutive stature, took Horr to task. It was a long and well-thought-
out response, which in part is as follows (Boykin 1961, 66–68):

> Was it logical for my friend the other day to call the attention of the House
> to my body? Suppose I am little, was it logical, or parliamentary, or kind to
> say it? . . . I represent large folks, fighting folks, *(laughter)* good folks; they
> did not measure my girth or take my altitude when they sent me here. . . .
> They did not think blubber indicated brains; nor meat manhood. . . . They
> did not regard me as unworthy of their trust, because I had not layers of lard
> over immense abdominal muscles *(Prolonged laughter.)* They are intelligent;
> they know that tissues of fat do not control issues of fact or politics. . . . Sup-
> pose he be six feet high and have an abdomen ten feet in girth. Does the gen-
> tleman tell me that therefore he can assume airs of superiority, 'genial' airs?
> Suppose he has a longer oscoxygis *(laughter)* and his ancestors had a firmer
> prehensile grip to a Darwinian limb. *(Great laughter)* Perhaps next he will
> raise the point of order on me that I cannot vote because my esophagus is
> not as magnificent as his own *(laughter)*, or his phalanges or metacarpus or,
> rather, corn-stealers, are bigger than those of any other member. *(Laughter.)*
> . . . Over his grave let there be inscribed:

> *Here lies the body*
> *of*
> *Congressman* Horr:
> *'Tis Greece,*
> *But*
> Living *Grease*
> *no more!*
> Requiescat!

Not to be outdone, Congressman Horr gamely struck back with poetry
provided to him, he said, by a friend:

> Beneath this slab lies the great SAM COX,
> He was wise as an owl and grave as an ox;
> Think it not strange his turning to dust,
> For he swelled and swelled he till finally "bust."
> Just where he's gone and how he fares,
> Nobody knows and nobody cares.
> But wherever his is, be he angel or elf,
> Be sure, dear friend, he's puffing himself. (Boykin 1961, 69)

Cox was not the only member of Congress to become irritated about condescending references to his height. Congressman Alexander Stephens (D-GA), who would become vice president of the Confederacy, stood only five feet tall and weighed but eighty pounds. While a "raw-boned" congressman from the Northwest was making his maiden speech, Stephens interrupted him several times. Finally, the Northwesterner lost control of his temper and "bellowed at his colleague, 'Why you little shrimp, I could eat you in one bite and I would not know that I had anything to eat.' To that, the fiery little Georgian drawled, 'If you did, you would have more brains in your belly than you now have in your head'" (Wiley 1947, 114).

Ridicule can be mutual play, but even then it can be risky. In these verbal jousts, one party might identify traits that make a caricature the other party. As a result, the play is not likely to be mutual but at the expense of one of the parties; thus, such an exchange often invites retaliation. One relevant instance involves Congressman Willard Vandiver (D-MO, 1897–1905). He decided to have some fun at the expense of Congressman Charles Grosvenor. Vandiver's own prominent characteristics were that he was exceptionally lean and lank, without an ounce of fat it was said, and that he sported a heavy mustache that drooped over his mouth; so, naturally, he was vulnerable to ridicule. In a speech on the floor, he several times referred to "the gentleman from Ohio." As previously arranged between himself and Speaker of the House Champ Clark, Vandiver was interrupted by Clark, who asked to which gentleman from Ohio Vandiver was referring. "This gave him the opportunity to indulge in the witticism he was seeking to perpetrate on General Grosvenor, and he responded, 'That particular gentleman from Ohio who looks like Santa Claus but talks like Satan.'" When Vandiver sat down, Grosvenor, who indeed had a snowy beard, snowy hair, and a ruddy complexion, rose to speak. "'Mr. Speaker,' he said, 'I have never prided myself on my personal appearance, but I am in no wise ashamed of it. The gentleman from Missouri violated the proprieties of debate by referring to it. I trust I may be permitted to say that, whatever my appearance may be, whenever I look on the other side and see the Gentleman from Missouri, I have abundant cause to thank God that I do not look like the skull-and-crossbones on a poison bottle in a druggist's window, and when people hear my voice they do not instinctively recall that old song, 'Hark! from the tombs a doleful sound'" (Boykin 1961, 156; Watson 1936, 39–40). There were rounds of laughter at Vandiver's expense.

Like skilled cartoonists, persons in this sort of play at times identify a pronounced characteristic of an individual, and the label sticks. For example, Congressman David De Armond (D-MO, 1891–1909) was known as a gloomy character, "as bitter a man as ever stood upon his feet to make a speech." When he spoke, "He cut and slashed to beat the band in every direction, and he was constantly and invariably sad, lugubrious, and melancholy. To listen to him one would have thought the whole country was going to demnition. One of the wags in the House dubbed him the 'Whangdoodle from Missouri.' 'Gone where woodbine twineth and the Whangdoodle mourneth her first born.' Ever after it was difficult for him to escape the sobriquet" (Watson 1936, 285–86).

Senator James E. Watson writes, "Ridicule skillfully wielded, is recognized as the most dangerous of all weapons" (1936, 38). One of the most celebrated cases of ridicule in the history of the U.S. Senate dramatically points to the dangers inherent in its use. In 1866, when Representative James G. Blaine (R-ME) referred to the "turkey-gobbler strut of Roscoe Conkling" (R-NY, who was known for his arrogance), poor Conkling was drawn forever more in cartoons as a strutting turkey cock. But, eighteen years later, when Blaine was running for president, Conkling was asked to campaign for him. His response: "No thank you. I don't engage in criminal practice" (Boller 1991, 194–96; Boykin 1961, 47–48; Schutz 1977a, 259–61; Watson 1936, 19). As it turned out, New York's Oneida County, home of Conkling and heavily Republican, did not support Blaine, and New York State was lost by fewer than one thousand votes, a loss that translated into a loss of electoral votes that ultimately cost Blaine the national election! (Watson 1936, 19). So go the dangers of ridicule in politics.

BEING POLITICALLY CORRECT

Ideas about the appropriate topics for humor in Congress have changed greatly over the years. We can get some idea of these changes by comparing the notions about political correctness in the works of two unusually astute students of humor who were members of the House and who wrote a little more than a century apart. Samuel Cox's book *Why We Laugh* first appeared in 1876, with a second edition appearing in 1880. Congressman Morris Udall's book *Too Funny to Be President* was published a little more than a century later in 1988.

As Cox surveys the contours of American humor, he concludes that any topic—bar none—was suitable for humor. This sweeping conception of appropriate topics for humor mirrors his own viewpoint. Indeed, he and his contemporaries would not have known what to make of the term *political correctness*. Cox writes:

> The American legislature, like the American everywhere else, is estopped by no subject when his sense of humor is aroused. Wherever there is a loud promise and a poor performance; whatever is out of place and time; whatever

deranges plans and disturbs calculations; whenever there is a break in logical or sentimental continuity; whenever any thing appears fragmentary or abortive; whenever there is any thing mean, skulking, or delinquent; whenever dignity is oninionative, dumpish, or diabolical; whenever good principles are espoused by faulty and false folks; and whether the subject be serious or mirthful, scientific or superficial, the American will have his jibe and joke, and his mercurial temper overflows at once with its perception. ([1880] 1969, 319–20)

Cox believed that the distinctive characteristic of American humor was its wild exaggeration: it was raucous and therefore devoid of boundaries. His book includes humor about genders, race, and ethnicity—indeed, an entire chapter about Irish humor, for which he had much admiration. Cox also believed that others' physical and behavioral characteristics and differences were appropriate targets for humor: "These personalities are a piquant kind of humor which often becomes caustic wit. It touches the peculiar vocations, personal foibles, or physical peculiarities of members. This is not the highest order of festive legislation, but it is often used. Every one laughs at a hit about personal obliquities in body or mind" (192). However, his volcanic reaction to Congressman Horr's reference to him as "my genial little friend" made it abundantly clear that Cox did not appreciate others making fun of his own appearance![2]

A century later, Congressman Morris Udall concludes his classic book on humor by offering guidelines on the use of humor for those who felt they were humor challenged. His advice leaves little doubt that those who wish to employ humor need to tow to some rather strict rules of political correctness (1988, chap. 14). After assuring his readers, first, that they could be good with humor if only they would work on their timing and delivery and, second, that they should not be afraid to steal humor of others, he offers more specific guidelines. First, one must be sensitive to the values of one's audience—what works with one group may not work with another. Next, one needs to avoid smug jokes—that is, zingers aimed at others. Rather, one should tell self-deprecating jokes. At a time when so many topics are off-limits, a humorist is probably still safe in telling jokes at one's own expense. He goes on to admonish would-be humorists who fail to avoid racist and ethnic jokes: "Sacred cows make great hamburgers, but its only common sense for a public servant to avoid jokes with ethnic or racist overtones" (195). He quotes the political columnist Mark Shields: "With all of today's caucuses and groups, you're not permitted to be nearly as ethnic in your humor. . . . There are no Pedro, Pat or Manny stories being told. You *can* make fun of your own group, but you can't make fun of anybody else's. The one group you can make fun of is WASPS. They're fair game. . . . Remember, there is no Episcopalian Antidefamation League. I've checked" (196, emphasis in original). And, of course, sexist jokes are beyond the pale for would-be, late-twentieth-century congressional humorists. Women vote; they are organized; and they often decide elections with their convictions about feminist issues. Blatantly sexist humor is likely to invite electoral reprisals. Further, Udall advises that would-be humorists use topical humor. For this point, he again quotes Mark Shields: "If you make reference to something that happened between the salad and the soup, it works" (198). In short, jokes about politicians from even the recent past are not likely to tickle too many "ribs of joviality." The final principle for good humor is this: be gentle when employing humor. "Effective humor is never cruel, ridiculing, or belittling" (198). For all the world, this sounds like Sunset Cox a century earlier, when he wrote that "no malicious man was great either in wit or humor" (151). Similar as the words sound, they each had significantly different meanings derived from their historical contexts.

CONCLUSION

The use of congressional humor dates to the beginning of Congress itself. The nature of humor has changed over time, evolving with the times and with the institution and its membership. Those members who have been known to be skilled humorists, irrespective of the times, believe not only that speeches sprinkled with mirth are more memorable but that the deliverers themselves have a gift of great value that can make an audience eagerly anticipate what they have to say. Weighty arguments could be enlivened with the appropriate use of stories and spontaneous witticisms; contentious committee meetings could be defused with just the right infusion of humor. Those who are adept at creating and using humor share in common with most other members of Congress outstanding language skills, and at times their humor has been created through the use of exceptional language facility. However, it is more than this; it is also the facility to play with ideas to lay bare their striking discontinuities and similarities.

Using humor in politics is a bit like balancing on a high wire: it is exhilarating when you are successful, but if you make a misstep, you can fall a long way and get badly hurt. Humor can be misunderstood or taken out of context, and it can be given a meaning far from what was intended. Again, humor can detract from the message and one never wants to be seen as trying too hard to be funny or, worse yet, as simply being foolish. Indeed, there are those who feel that public discussion is too serious an activity to be sullied with humor.

Much humor depends on context for its effect. To appreciate it, one must know something about ongoing relationships, see facial expressions and gestures, and bare witness to the careful use of timing and delivery.

Spontaneous humor is often unmemorable because it is so dependent on time and place and because it soon loses its meaning. Ideas of political correctness depend on popular attitudes that change over time. Samuel Cox believed that no topic was an inappropriate target for humor, even personal characteristics; Morris Udall, however, advised politicians of his generation to be much more circumspect in their use of humor. For politicians in the latter generation, stories they used to regale audiences in the early days of their public careers are now seen as insensitive, even boorish.

Such have been the prospects and pitfalls for congresspersons who would attempt to spice up their work with humor.

NOTES

1. The eight members of Congress include Samuel S. Cox (D), who served in the House of Representatives from 1857 to 1865 (Ohio) and from 1869 to 1885 (New York); James Beauchamp "Champ" Clark (D-MO), who served in the House from 1893 to 1895 and from 1897 to 1921; James E. Watson (R-IN), who served in the House from 1895 to 1897 and from 1899 to 1909 and in the Senate from 1916 to 1933; Alben W. Barkley (D-KY), who served in the House of Representatives from 1913 to 1927, in the Senate from 1927 to 1949 and from 1955 to 1956, and as vice president from 1949 to 1953; Alexander Wiley (R-WI), who served in the Senate from 1939 to 1963; Sam J. Ervin Jr. (D-NC), who served in the House during 1946 to 1947 and in the Senate from 1954 to 1974; Representative Brooks Hays (D-AR), who served from 1943 until 1959; and Representative Morris Udall (D-AZ), who served from 1961 to 1991. To our knowledge, Watson and Wiley were not known to be great wits in their own right, but they certainly were skilled chroniclers and students of humor.

2. Some insight into the state of political correctness as late as 1933 might be garnered from the choice of stories of freshman congressman Everett McKinley Dirksen. He was given the oath of office on March 9, 1933. Less than two weeks later, he made his maiden speech, announcing he represented the district that Abraham Lincoln had represented in 1846. He then "rattled off" a number of stories, perhaps to show that he was a proper heir to the master storyteller's district. He first told a story about a couple of army chaplains who were lost during World War I. They were wandering around in mud and shell holes when they heard a voice from the trench say, "Who in hell led that ace?" The chaplains got up and embraced each other and said, "Thank goodness, we are among Christians." Another story Dirksen told involved a "Negro lady" who had bought a pair of stockings that did not fit, so she returned them to the store. The clerk asked, "What is the matter—didn't they come up to your expectations?" "Lawsy, boss, they do not even come up to my knees." He then went on to tell an Irish joke. An Irishman had fallen on the steps of the House office building. "He had a bottle of that good old Maryland rye in his hip pocket. He fell down, and as he got up he felt something

trickling down his leg, and he said, 'Begorra! And I hope its blood.'" A few days later in addressing a reciprocal trade bill he told a story about a "little colored boy who sat among a pile of watermelons with distended stomach, unable to eat any more. Some kindly gentleman came long and asked, 'What's the matter, too much melon?' The little boy said, 'Nope, too little nigger.'" (This is one of the few uses of the "N" word that we found in the public [as opposed to private] humor of congresspersons.) Thus, within a few weeks of the time he was sworn in, he had managed to aim his humor at African Americans, women, religion, and ethnic groups! (All of these stories come from MacNeil 1970, 52–53). It is a revealing commentary on attitudes prevalent in the early 1930s that this skilled storyteller made a calculation that these stories would be well received by his audience and would aid him and his message gain acceptance.

3

Humorous Stories and the Identification of Social Norms: The Senate Club

Sinitoryal courtesy rules th' body. If ye let me talk I'll let ye sleep.

—Mr. Dooley, in *Dissertations by Mr. Dooley* (Finley Peter Dunne)

In some ways legislative bodies such as the U.S. Senate can be compared to formal organizations such as bureaucracies or large private organizations. Students of formal organizations stress the importance of informal structures and how such structures influence the behavior of an organization's members (March and Olsen 1989; Martin 1992; Meyer and Rowan 1977; Ott 1989). One particular aspect of informal structure that has caught observers' attention is storytelling (Hummel 1991; Martin and Powers 1983; Mitroff and Kilmann 1975; Ott 1989; Wilkins 1983). Stories are told and retold and hence passed from old members to new. Such stories are held to be important to organizations for two reasons: first, because information that is acquired in story form is more easily remembered; and, second, because information presented in stories is more likely to generate belief and commitment by members of the organization than that presented in other formats (Hummel 1991; Martin and Powers 1983; Wilkins 1983). Thus, they contribute to a formal organization's control over its members (Wilkins 1983; Martin and Powers 1983; Mitroff and Kilmann 1975). For example, some of these stories amount to scripts that teach approved behavior to members of the organization (Martin and Powers 1983; Ott 1989; Wilkins 1983). Scholars believe that stories told in organizations form an important type of data for seeing the world as seen by organizational participants and for understanding such participants' behavior. If we are to understand the actions of legislative leaders in their respective institutional settings, it stands to reason that stories passed on to new members should be equally revealing. In this chapter, I examine humorous stories that have been passed along in the U.S. Senate during the years of the "Senate Club." I compare the "scripts," or prescriptions, suggested in these stories to the norms discussed by Donald R. Matthews in his classic book *U.S. Senators and Their World* (1960), which identifies norms of the Senate during the time of the Senate Club.

Whereas scholars of organizations emphasize how stories contribute to order in formal organizations, scholars of humor discuss the playful and ambiguous nature of humor, as well as its penchant for satire and sarcasm, as a potential source of change. Murray Davis, for example, offers this insight: "Sociologists have distinguished typical individuals, groups, roles, institutions and even 'realities' as major units of the social world; and have been trying to determine their essential characteristics" (1993, 217). However, "Comics try to discover whether it provokes a laugh to contradict what they hypothesize to be an essential characteristic of a typical social unit. Specifically, they replace this hypothesized essential characteristic with another feature (from a different social unit) they believe so uncharacteristic that imagining it together with the first unit's other features will be laughable" (217). Davis goes onto assert that comics "are social scientists whose methods are merely indirect" (217).

Developing the perspective that the existing social structure must allow for the joke to be perceived, Mary Douglas echoes Davis's point: "My hypothesis is that a joke is seen and allowed when it offers a symbolic pattern of a social pattern occurring at the same time. As I see it, all jokes are expressive of the social situations in which they occur. The one social condition necessary for a joke to be enjoyed is that the social group in which it is received should develop the formal characteristics of the 'told' joke: that is, a dominant pattern of relations is challenged by another. If there is no joke in the social structure, no other joking can appear" (1975, 98).

Scholars of humor cited to this point see humor as important only in challenging norms. Others see humor as playing a major role, both in protecting norms and promoting social control, as well as in challenging norms and thus portending conflict and change. Addressing both of these outcomes, sociologist Richard Stephenson writes, "The conflict function of humor is expressed largely by means of irony, satire, sarcasm, caricature, parody, burlesque, and the like. The particular adaptability of humor as a conflict weapon lies in the fact that humor may conceal malice and allow expression of aggression without the consequences of other overt behavior. . . . As a means of social control, humor may function to express approval or disapproval of social form and action, express common group sentiments, develop and perpetuate stereotypes, relieve awkward or tense situations, and express collective, *sub rosa* approbation of action not explicitly approved" (1951, 569–70). Similarly, Joyce Hertzler contends that humor both supports and augures for change in the status quo. To the topic of humor as a reinforcer of norms, he writes, "In the last analysis, laughter as a conservative agent has its ultimate effect on the individual. If he swings out too far in dress, or speech, or extreme behavior of any kind, the laughter of his fellows engulfs him and often chastens him. But there is a broader social aspect. Social laughter often is an expression of criticism, even outrage, by the herd against the maverick, or the independent" (1970, 120). But Hertzler also speaks to the change functions of humor: "This renovative function is that of the ridiculing, cynical, or skeptical laughter which routs out and parodies and criticizes worn-out or false ideas, and beliefs, and ideologies, repressive or restrictive social codes, outmoded or stereotyped proprieties and ways of life, archaic or petrified institutional forms, organizational rigidities, inelasticities of habit, customs, conventions, rituals, and ceremonies. . . . Critical humor, employing the various laughter-evoking devices, is widely resorted to as a means of revealing sick spots and dead ends and hardening of the arteries—of showing up what is wrong" (120–21). In an attempt to develop a model of the social functions of humor, another sociologist, William Martineau, hypothesizes that humor, depending on the circumstances, can lead to either intragroup cohesion or conflict (Martineau 1972, 114–24).

The implication of the playful, ambiguous, and critical nature of humor is that while humorous stories are often relevant to group norms, they can either support or challenge them as well. The central point for this research is that humorous stories contain prescriptions that relate to an institution's culture, by either attacking or supporting established norms.

SENATE NORMS

Matthews's study of Senate folkways is of interest to us because it seeks to show how informal aspects of the institution affect the behavior of senate members. His work is based on 109 interviews—approximately a quarter of which are with current and recent members of the Senate (most of the remainer are with staff members)—and on material taken from news sources and past members' biographies and autobiographies. The data, largely anecdotal, are rich and instructive. The Senate that Matthews portrays is an orderly, nigh, a civil place in which a member can learn the informal norms that guide behavior. These norms render behavior understandable and predictable. Matthews not only describes the Senate institution of the time, but he also demonstrates a prescience as to what sorts of developments would lead to the institution's eventual change (1960, 102–17).[1]

Matthews identifies six folkways, or norms, of the Senate: "The first rule of Senate behavior, and the one most widely recognized off the Hill, is that new members are expected to serve a proper apprenticeship" (92). The second Senate norm is "legislative work." "There are two kinds of Congressmen—show horses and work horses" (94). In short, to hold the respect of their colleagues, members must carry their share of the burden of legislative work. The third norm is "specialization." The idea here is that a senator ought "to focus his energy and attention on the relatively few matters that come before his committees or that directly and immediately affect his state" (95). Next comes the norm of "courtesy." This norm simply provides that members of the Senate should not personalize issues: "Personal attacks, unnecessary unpleasantness, and pursuing a line of thought or action that might embarrass a colleague needlessly are thought to be self-defeating—'After all, your enemies on one issue may be your friends on the next'" (98). The fifth norm discussed by Matthews is "reciprocity," which provides that senators ought to extend reasonable courtesies to their colleagues, where possible. Among other things, this means Senators try to understand and be sympathetic to the problems of other members, that they keep their explicit and implicit commitments, and that they not use all the powers to which individual Senators are entitled under the rules of the Senate (99–101). Finally, there is the norm of "institutional patriotism": "A Senator whose emotional commitment to Senate ways appears to be less than total is suspect" (102). All together, these are work norms that one would expect to find in a task-oriented organization.

The folkways, or norms, that Matthews discovered are passed along by an oral tradition. New members would not find them by consulting *Jefferson's Rules*. Rather, new members are instructed, if at all, by older members of the Senate as to the institution's norms and expectations; otherwise, new members simply learn through personal observation. A part of the oral tradition in Congress is the passing along of humorous stories. James E. Watson, who was majority leader of the Senate during the Hoover administration, commented on this: "Naturally, there are stories without number extant, handed down, as it were, from generation to generation of members of Congress, until they have become a part of the tradition of that body" (1936, 41). Stephen Young (D-OH, 1959–1971) had not been in the Senate more than five days when he was approached by a member of that institution. "'You may have heard that the Senate of the United States is the most exclusive club in the world. I want to tell you about a really exclusive club. We call it the Hideaway and our membership committee has unanimously elected you.' I was glad to join for when the Senate session is unduly prolonged, there is usually a relaxed club meeting. Senator Maurine Neuberger is welcome. Senators Everett Jordan, Sam Ervin, Dick Russell and Herman Talmage are about the best story tellers" (1964, 62). The importance of these stories is not their factual accuracy; indeed, as they have been told and retold, it is likely that they have been embellished and shaped to make the appropriate points. Occasionally, they have been committed to writing and are thus important sources of information about the institution. In this chapter, I explore the value of prescriptions contained in humorous stories as an alternative kind of data to identify legislative norms. Specifically, the questions I pose are thus: First, can we identify the Senate norms that Matthews identifies, by drawing on the oral tradition of repeating humorous stories about past members and incidents in the Senate? Second, would the scripts contained in these stories suggest some additional norms? Matthews's work provides an ideal baseline for this study because enough time has passed since he wrote in that several books written by senators, about senators, and about the Senate have appeared to provide us with appropriate data.

Matthews' Norms and Humorous Stories

To address these research questions, I have analyzed humorous stories found in ten sources: six books by members of the Congress who were known to be skilled users of humor or who were students of congressional humor, two books by noted historians who collected and presented congressional wit and wisdom, and two joke books dealing with congressional humor.[2] In replicating Matthews's study, it is necessary to gather humor made during a time when the Senate was an institution comparable to that when Matthews studied it. Thus, the end point I chose for the inclusion of data is 1960 (the publication date of Matthews's book), give or take a few years. I cannot be more precise than this because my sources do not always allow us to identify the precise time when a depicted humorous situation took place. It is unclear from Matthews's work what starting point frames his study. Most of the data he gathered came from the 1950s. However, he cites senators whose tenure in the institution predates that by several decades. In at least one case, he cites the sagely advice of George Washington (1960, 117n). Moreover, the origin of the norms he discusses is uncertain. To research our questions, we examine, for the most part, data that originate from 1920 and after. It seems safe to say that these years, 1920 to 1960, are years in which the Senate was the clubby place that Matthews describes. Not all stories that are passed along as part of the oral tradition are humorous, and not all humorous stories suggest prescriptions about behavior or attitudes toward the institution. Some stories are retold simply because of their clever play on words, their powerful put-downs, or their juxtaposition of concepts. In this study, I focus on those humorous stories that do suggest scripts about proper behavior and appropriate attitudes toward the Senate. Table 3.1 shows how well we are able to identify the same norms Matthews identified when we use humorous stories.

One norm, apprenticeship, is not the object of any humorous stories. Does this mean that apprenticeship is not a senate norm? Not really. Some nonhumorous anecdotes do point to the existence of this norm. For example, one story is about Senator John Kennedy, when he was a freshman senator. After a frenetic day in which, among other activities, he held a news conference, offered several amendments to pending legislation, and spoke on two or three bills, he "collapsed" in a chair next to Senator Carl Hayden (who had been a member of the Senate for more than forty years) and began to make small talk: "'Well, 'I guess you must have seen lots of changes in the time you've been here.' 'Yes,' said Hayden curtly. 'What were some of the more important ones?' Kennedy asked. 'Well,' said Hayden, 'for one thing, in those days, freshman senators didn't talk'" (Udall 1988, 106–7; also cited in Boller 1991, 221). This story also appears in Matthews (1960, 94); however, the freshman senator is not identified, and the elder member is Senator George (D-GA). Another similar story involves Senator Borah (R-ID), who served in the Senate from 1907 to 1940, on the occasion of his being eulogized on his birthday. When a freshman senator who had been in the Senate only a few months gave a speech praising Borah, the latter uttered in a loud whisper, "that son-of-a-bitch, that son-of-a-bitch.' 'He didn't dislike the man personally. He just didn't think he should be making a speech so soon'" (Matthews 1959, 1066; see also, Boller 1991, 209; Matthews 1960, 93–94). While carrying clear messages about the institution and the role of new members in it, these instances can hardly be classified as funny. Why are there no humorous stories about the norm of apprenticeship? It may be that the norm just does not lend itself to good humor.

In our data pool, three humorous renderings relate to each of the norms of legislative work and specialization. Regarding the former, minority floor leader Hugh Scott read a tongue-in-cheek letter to JFK about how proud his fellow senators were when Kennedy gave his brilliant speech on leadership at his college reunion at Harvard and then appeared on the Jack Paar Show offering many witticisms. Senators who gave up a chance

Table 3.1. Replication of Matthews's Norms Using Humorous Incidents

Type of Norm	#Norms
Apprenticeship	0
Legislative work	3
Specialization	3
Courtesy	16
Reciprocity	11
Institutional patriotism	6

to mend fences in their states, to give speeches to large groups, and (in one case) to receive an honorary degree stayed in Washington to do the institution's "heavy lifting" and eagerly awaited Kennedy's return, to see him attempt to exercise leadership in the very institution that the other senators believed he neglected. He ended his spoof letter, "Well, we don't want to bore you, Jack. If you have time, drop in and if not, just send one of the other Kennedys down" (Gingras 1973, 13–15).

On the topic of specialization, Hogan and Hill cite a story told by Senator A. Willis Robertson (D-VA): "Once upon an occasion, a stranger was traveling in Scotland, and he said to a Scotsman, 'Is this the road to Edinburgh?' The Scotsman said, 'Yes my friend, but you will have to turn around'" (39–40). Also relevant to specialization is one of the many stories that Senator Alben Barkley told about his "Uncle Zeke," who was renowned for his wisdom. When asked why he was so wise, Uncle Zeke said, "Waal, I've got good judgement. Good judgement comes from experience; and experience . . . waal that comes from bad judgement" (Udall 1988, 200; also cited in Boller 1991, 162).

The remaining three norms identified by Matthews are also verified by several humorous renderings: courtesy, with sixteen references; reciprocity, with eleven; and institutional patriotism, with six. A couple of examples of each suffice to convey the character of these norms. In a section of his book entitled "Some Random Notes," Alben Barkley offers this anecdote regarding courtesy: "This is confidential among us senators. If you think one of your colleagues is stupid in debate, which you will think if you are here long, refer to him as 'the able, learned and distinguished senator.' If you *know* he is stupid, which you probably will, refer to him as 'the *very* able, learned and distinguished senator.' This form of address conceals a multitude of shortcomings" (1954, 255, emphasis in original).[3] Another instance relevant to senatorial courtesy is the nomination of Clare Boothe Luce, former congresswoman and noted conservative, to be ambassador to Brazil. When it came up, Senator Dirksen rose to defend her from Democrats who recalled her several past uncharitable comments about FDR. "'Why thrash old straws', he cried 'or beat an old bag of bones?' As the Senators began laughing at Dirksen's unfortunate phrase, Democrat Hubert Humphrey leaped to his feet and cried mischievously: 'I must rise to the defense of the lady.' 'I am referring to the old bag of political bones,' stammered Dirksen in embarrassment. Mrs. Luce won confirmation, but resigned when a crack she took at Senator Wayne Morse, one of her opponents, angered most of the Senators" (Boller 1991, 168; see also MacNeil 1970, 157).

As noted earlier, humor both challenges and affirms norms; the essential concern for inclusion in our data is that humor addresses norms. Then again, what appears to be criticism to some can, from a different perspective, be a defense of the institution and its norms. The incidents dealing with senators' reciprocity often take the form of their criticizing other senators for not keeping their word or for their trying to be on both sides of an issue. This motive is evident in an exchange between Senator Thomas Heflin (D-AL) and Senator Kenneth D. McKellar (D-TN). Heflin offered this story: "It reminds me of the old fellow out in Texas who wrote back to a friend in Tennessee. He said: 'Dear Bill: If you have not started for Texas, don't. This is the most hellacious climate in the world. Only yesterday, while driving a yoke of steers across the prairie, one of them had a sunstroke and while I was skinning him, the other one froze to death.' That was a quick change in the weather, Mr. President, but not much quicker than the changes of my friend from Tennessee" (Boykin 1961, 30). Another similar story involves an exchange between Senator Everett Dirksen and Senator Lyndon Johnson. Dirksen, tired of Johnson's frequent and misleading use of statistics, commented that statements made by the majority leader were all right so far as they went. "However, it is like the man who fell off the twentieth floor of a building. As he passed the sixth floor, a friend shouted, 'Mike, so far you're alright'" (Boykin 1961, 19; see also Udall 1988, 146). Dirksen commented that he believed in the whole of the story, rather than a fraction.

The norm of institutional patriotism refers to the reverence in which its members hold the institution. Sometimes this is expressed with outright praise and sometimes as ironic humor. In the latter vein is an oft-told tale involving a former chaplain to the Senate, Edward Everett Hale. When asked if he prayed for the Senate, he commented, "No, I look at the Senators and pray for the country" (Wiley 1947, 59; see also, Boller 1991, 19, who notes that this story has become generic; Gingras 1973, 70).[4] During the hearings to censure Senator Joe McCarthy, Senator Ervin told the following anecdote to show that McCarthy's behavior was harmful to the Senate:

> Mr. President, many years ago there was a tradition in a section of my county, known as the South Mountains, to hold religious meetings at which the oldest members of the congregation were called upon to stand up and publicly testify to their religious experiences. On one occasion they were holding such a meeting in one of the churches, and old Uncle Ephraim Swink, a South Mountaineer whose body was bent and distorted with arthritis, was present. All the older members of the congregation except Uncle Ephraim arose and gave testimony to their religious experiences. Uncle Ephrain kept his seat. Thereupon the moderator said, "Brother Ephraim, suppose you tell us what the Lord has done for you." Uncle Ephraim arose with his bent and distorted body, and said, "Brother, he has mighty nigh ruint me." Mr. President, that is about what Senator McCarthy has done to the Senate. (Ervin 1983, 162–63; see also, Boller 1991, 142; Udall 1988, 228)

Humorous Stories and Other Norms

The remaining question that we set for ourselves at the outset of this chapter is, Are there norms that Matthews does not single out that are suggested through the use of humorous stories? As indicated by table 3.2, there are important Senate norms that fit this description. These include norms against long-windedness (twenty-one references), in support of comity (ten references), against alcoholism (eight references), and one other that we shall call *leveling* (eighteen references).

Matthews does discuss the dangers of long-windedness for the institution. When he identifies five functions of the norms, the second one is that they discourage senators' long-windedness (Matthews 1960, 102). Moreover, when he discusses reciprocity, one of the meanings he gives it is that if a senator does not push his or her formal powers to the limit, he or she can expect that other senators will reciprocate (101). However, Matthews never chooses to isolate long-windedness as a separate norm.

Our data clearly show that extended debate, the threat of extended debate, or even simply long-windedness are taken seriously in much humor; and that having the reputation of being long-winded was something that senators would do well to avoid. For example, Senator Borah (R-ID) was usually an interesting and popular speaker. Word that he was speaking would bring members to the floor and reporters to the gallery. However, sometimes he would belabor a point and become ponderous. "During one of his overlong harangues a weary Senator slipped out of the Senate chamber and headed for the cloakroom. 'How is Borah's speech going?' one of his colleagues asked. 'Just fine', sighed the Senator. 'When I left he was reaching new heights of Borahdom'" (Boller 1991, 97).

An interaction between Senator Reynolds (D-NC) and floor leader Alben Barkley sheds light on the norm against long-windedness:

> The gentleman from North Carolina had a well-known proclivity for making long and discursive speeches, especially if he knew that any of his constituents were in the gallery. If he had nothing particular to say, he would go on about beautiful and interesting places he had visited throughout the

Table 3.2. Norms Other Than Those
Found by Matthews, Identified by Use
of Humorous Incidents

Type of Norm	#Norms
Anti-long-windedness	21
Comity	10
Anti-alcoholism	8
Leveling	18

world. One day Senator Reynolds had been on his feet a long time; he had quite exhausted the natural beauties of the Far West and was headed for the islands of the Pacific. As majority leader, I had some business I wanted to get accomplished, so I tapped him on the shoulder and said, "Senator, let me off when you get to Shanghai." (Barkley 1954, 272; Boller 1991, 163; for a similar characterization of Senator Wayne Morse [I-OR], see Gingras 1973, 136)

Matthews does not discuss the relation of the maverick to the Senate as an institution when he discusses senate norms. Senator Huey Long (D-LA), who served in the Senate from 1932 to 1935, is as good of an example of a maverick as one can hope to find. As a new member of the Senate, he resigned from committee assignments if he was not interested in the work of the committees. He purposely picked a fight with the senior senator from his state so that he could be escorted to take the oath of office by Joe Robinson (D-AR). The "Kingfish," as he was called, violated rules by carrying a lit cigar to the front, which he placed on the clerk's desk while he took the oath. "Afterward, when he was presented to William E. Borah, he embraced him heartily, to Borah's astonishment; . . . and went on to treat everyone boisterously, galloping around the Senate chamber, it was said, 'like a colt turned out to pasture'" (Boller 1991, 55–56). Senator James Watson writes about when he first met Long: "My acquaintance with that spectacular Senator known to all Americans as Huey Long began one day when he came up to me on the floor of the Senate, gave me a smashing blow with his open hands on my chest which staggered me backward, and said to me in an explosive fashion: 'Jim, I want to get acquainted with you.' Taken aback at this treatment, I exclaimed, 'Who in the hell are you?' 'I,' he responded, 'am Huey Long'" (1936, 304).

Though Huitt (1957, 1961) and White (1956, 121–33) in their works contend that members of the "inner club" of the Senate placed a high value on freedom of thought and individualism and that they were careful to distinguish between the expression of ideas and obstructive behavior, the instances here show that these members of the "world's greatest deliberative body" did not in an unqualified way welcome prolonged speech. Why should they? They were task oriented, and endless speech got in the way of legislative accomplishments. And when the member in question was the roguish Senator Huey Long, members could be downright cruel, even at the level of speech. For example, Long took delight in stirring up Vice President John Garner, and it was known that Garner had little respect for him. "One day after he had made himself particularly offensive to the chair, Huey jumped up for about the fiftieth time and in a bantering voice said: 'Mr. President, I rise to make a parliamentary inquiry. . . . How should a senator, who is half in favor of this bill and half against it, cast his vote?'

Garner glowered at him from beneath his bushy white eyebrows and said: 'Get a saw and saw yourself in two; that's what you ought to do anyhow'" (Barkley 1954, 159). During Long's famous filibuster in 1935—in which Long held forth for fifteen and a half hours and in which he read his recipe for potlikker soup, went into detail about how to fry oysters, and even read the U.S. Constitution verbatim—Long received much verbal abuse from other senators. Note this exchange between Barkley and Long:

MR. LONG: Very well, I had that coming to me. I remember when I first tried to study music; they gave me a poor grade.

MR. BARKLEY: Did the Senator learn music?

MR. LONG: Not much of it; a little.

MR. BARKLEY: Will not the Senator sing a little? [Laughter.]

MR. LONG: Mr. President. The Senator wants me to sing to him. There may be some people I will sing to, but they will be better looking than the Senator from Kentucky. [Laughter.]

MR. BARKLEY: The Senator will never sing looking in a looking glass then, if that be true. (Hogan and Hill 1987, 68)

Even Senator Carter Glass (D-VA) couldn't resist sarcasm where Huey Long was concerned. "Senator Glass remarked that the Senate of the United States had surpassed Caligula in making his horse a consul; it had made the posterior of a horse a U.S. Senator" (Schutz 1977a, 251, see also, Boller 1991, 98).[5]

One Senate norm that turns up in our study but is not included in Matthews's study is the norm of comity. By *comity,* I mean courtesies extended either by one branch to members of the other coequal branches; or by one chamber of Congress to the other (Yarwood 1981, 330–31; and Yarwood 1993, 658–60). Humorous stories about relations between the two chambers frequently reflect the chambers' competitive nature and quite often illustrate a bantering nature. For example, one of Senator Wiley's favorite stories is from Senator Claude Pepper (D-FL), who recalled a dream had by Speaker Reed:

Reed said one night he dreamed that the Congress had amended the Constitution and provided a new method of electing a President. The new method was that the President should be elected by a secret ballot of Senators. The momentous day arrived when the proposal was to be tried out for the first time. The galleries were naturally filled. The representatives of the press stood by intently to see what would be the result of the first trial of the new method of electing a President. Finally the golden urns were passed up to the Presiding Officer to be canvassed. While everyone listened with bated breath, the result was announced, and it was discovered that every Senator had one vote. (Wiley 1947, 24)

In another one of Wiley's stories, "Senators and Representatives were having a joint luncheon. Most of the group were on the last course—the dessert. One Senator was observed, however, still on the appetizer course, strumming his fingers against the table and muttering oaths. 'What's the matter, Tom?' asked a colleague, 'why don't you help yourself to some more of the vittles?' 'I have been waiting for my food from those blankety blank Representatives at the far end. You know how long it takes the House to pass anything'" (1947, 13). In another story, "A representative's wife shook her sleeping husband vigorously. 'Wake up, John,' she whispered excitedly, 'there's a robber in the house.' 'Nonsense, my dear,' was the husband's response. 'In the Senate, yes, but in the House, never'" (1947, 13).

Not only do norms protect members of the group and the organization from threats that would undo its members, but they also facilitate the actual work of the organization. Alcoholism is a continual threat to legislators because of the nonstop round of social life in which they can be engaged. Senator Stephen Young (D-OH), in his *Tales out of Congress* writes, "Frankly, unless a Senator throws in the sponge and accepts only one-fourth of the invitations, he will be out socially for five or six evenings weekly" (1964, 47). He mentions the numerous embassy receptions, the state dinners, the invitations to functions from an endless number of pressure groups, the Washington social soirees, as well as the frequent luncheons and dinners with constituents. Matthews himself relates the oft-told story of Senator Theodore Green (D-RI) who looked at his appointment book while at a social function. "'Senator Green,' his colleague asked, 'are you looking in your book to see where you go next?' 'No,' he replied, 'I am trying to find out where I am now'" (1960, 80; see also, Boller 1991, 66; Ervin 1983, 180–81; and Udall 1988, 200). The dangers of excessive drinking and a loose social life are recognized. For example, Barkley warns, "If on official trips, you put bay rum on your expense account, then, put it in your hair. Otherwise, it is petty graft" (Barkley 1954, 255). Senator John Sharp Williams (D-MS), who served in the House and Senate from 1893 to 1923, was noted for his heavy drinking: "One day Williams came into the Senate about 3:00 and started down the aisle while Senator J. Thomas Heflin, of Alabama, was making a speech. . . . He stepped into the aisle and caught a sentence or two of Mr. Heflin's speech and made a sarcastic remark in response. Whereupon Senator Heflin sarcastically exclaimed: 'Well, whatever else may be said of me, when I come to the Senate chamber, I always come in full possession of my faculties.' 'Well,' Williams flashed back, 'what difference does that make?'" (Watson 1936, 287–88;

see also, Boller 1991, 209; Wiley 1947, 117). Wiley received a story from Senator Robert A. Taft (R-OH) who recalled an inebriated colleague's reporting his paired vote, "Mr. President, if my disting—if my disting—my dear colleague were here, he would vote 'nay' and were I here, I would vote 'aye'" (1947, 79). In another story, "One morning, a legendary Senator is supposed to have met a constituent, who, eager to please his legislator, asked 'Have you had any breakfast?' The Senator replied dryly, 'Not a drop'" (Wiley 1947, 16).[6] In passing it should be noted that the drunk in popular culture is often the object of grudging admiration because he violates rules of good sense and gets away with it. The same strain of thought toward drinking seemed to exist in the Senate.

The final norm we uncover in our effort to replicate the work of Matthews is that of leveling, which addresses the problem of boundaries between one's membership in an elite institution and one's electoral requirements. On the one hand, senators are members of one of the most select institutions in the world; on the other, they are dependent on the votes of some of the least of the least, to maintain their membership in that august body. This results in a continual tension between one's activities in the Senate and one's electoral activities. A cardinal sin is to become puffed up and arrogant. The form this sort of humor takes is that a senator goes back to his or her state soliciting votes from poor folks and, in the interaction, is "bested" by an uneducated dirt farmer or a poor old widow who is nigh onto senility. A couple of examples illustrate the point. The first is submitted to Wiley by Senators Guy Gillette (R-IA) and William Fulbright (D-AR). "As Senator Gillette tells it, as it happened to him, his colored maid had noticed that the Senator, then a Representative, had his picture in the newspaper. Underneath was a caption to the effect that he might be nominated for the Upper Chamber. 'Is a Senatuh higher than a Congressman?' the maid asked. 'Yes,' answered Gillette, 'they are so considered because a Senator represents an entire state and a Representative represents a District of the state.' The maid's next question was: 'Well, is there anything lower than a Congressman?' Gillette answered that in most people's opinion, there was indeed nothing lower than a Congressman" (Wiley 1947, 14). Another story involving leveling comes from Lyndon Johnson while he was majority leader of the Senate. "Once . . . one of his constituents came to ask a favor and pointed out he had voted time and again for LBJ in his races for the House and Senate. 'So naturally,' said Johnson, 'Ah thanked the man for his fine support' and Ah said, 'Ma friend, what can Ah do for you?' and mah visitor said, 'Well, Senator, after all Ah did to hepp you, Ah wonder if you could hepp me become a citizen?'" (Boller 1991, 133). United States senators expect to stir up some excitement and draw some attention when they visit small towns around their state, but it does not always turn out that way. Anticipating the usual reception, Senator Fred Hale, while visiting a small town in Maine, dropped into a local store and commenced to talk to its proprietor. "When someone came in and wanted a couple of yards of calico, the proprietor immediately started to wait on the customer. When he had finished, Hale started to talk again. Then someone came wanting a pound of butter and so on, and that went on for a dozen interruptions. Hale didn't seem to getting anywhere. At last he said: 'You don't seem to like me.' The old grocer replied, 'I don't like you; I don't dislike you; I don't give a darn about you'" (Wiley 1947, 223; see also Boller 1991, 21).

These four norms—regarding long-windedness, comity, alcoholism, and leveling—which are in addition to norms found by Matthews are important to the work of the Senate. Given the fast-paced social calendar of senate members, alcoholism is a constant threat to each senator's health and productivity. The Constitution provides that there be two chambers to the legislature and three branches of government and that law making requires cooperation among them; obviously helpful are some unofficial understandings about how that cooperation takes place. Members of the U.S. Senate belong to one of the most prestigious law-making bodies in the world; getting their comeuppance from constituents helps them to maintain their perspective. And finally, the Senate as a body is judged by its ability to accomplish legislative tasks that constituents want completed; it needs some way to nudge unnecessarily garrulous members to cut short their rambling speeches in the interest of getting on with the collective tasks at hand.

CONCLUSION

Stories are an important and overlooked source of data for the study of political institutions. In this study, we examined humorous stories passed down in the U.S. Senate that were extant when Matthews published his book, and we were able to identify most of the same norms that he had identified. In addition, humorous stories point to still other norms. In using humorous stories for this purpose, one finds it important to recognize the playful nature of humor. For this work, it meant looking for stories that contain scripts related to the institution's prescribed behavior or attitudes, including those with not necessarily approving themes. Humor allows members of organizations to be a bit irreverent without being disloyal, which is a statement true of political as well as bureaucratic organizations—that is, loyal members of the organization can also be *Dilbert* devotees. In addition, members' playfulness is an important source of change, as organization members spoof current arrangements and imagine alternative combinations by seeking and presenting incongruent associations among structures. This is true to some extent in all organizations, but, as has been frequently pointed out in the literature of political science, rules are an important determinative of who gets what, when, and how. Norms are a part of the political struggle and are thus subject to change through humor as well as through other means.

When we use stories told in political institutions as we have in this study, the data are obviously qualitative. To the methodological purist, this is less than rigorous research. However, politics is passion and emotion; it is people in institutions who share myths and rituals and who show solidarity within and between groups. To deal with such subjectivity, one needs to attempt to get into the heads of an institution's members, think as they think, and see the organization as they see it. Much of the subject matter of politics necessarily results from social construction, which is true also of the behavioral interpretations that scholars choose to share and accept as valid.

NOTES

1. The literature is quite extensive in dealing with the Senate's moving away from the "clubby" atmosphere prevalent of the time when Matthews wrote. This change apparently took place during the decades immediately after Matthews's book was published. See especially, the work of Alan Ehrenhalt (1982); Nancy Kassebaum (1988); Norman Ornstein, Robert Peabody, and David Rohde (1977, 1985); Steven Roberts (1984); Barbara Sinclair (1989); and Eric Uslaner (1993).

2. The books by members of Congress include those by Alben Barkley (1954), Sam Ervin Jr. (1983), Morris Udall (1988), James Watson (1936), Alexander Wiley (1947), and Stephen Young (1964). The books by historians are those by Paul Boller Jr. (1991) and Edward Boykin (1961), and the joke books are by Angele de T. Gingras (1973) and Bill Hogan and Mike Hill (1987). In terms of norms and institutional development, it is of interest to note how many of the humorous stories appear in several sources. The books included for analysis are the best known and most relevant books of their types, given the time frame of this study.

Some quantitatively inclined souls might argue that data could better be gathered by performing a content analysis of the *Congressional Record*. There are at least three problems with this. One problem is that a researcher would have to analyze an inordinate number of pages to find enough worthwhile humor. Of note is historian Edward Boykin, whose *Wit and Wisdom of Congress* is the most ambitious search undertaken for congressional humor of the *Record* and its predecessors, stretching as it does from 1789 until 1961. Boykin comments that he was not able to read every page of the written record of congressional proceedings to search out humor. Rather he "devised a homely method of scanning a volume and tapping what was best in it" (1961, v). Hardly the stuff of quantitative content analysis! A second problem with using the *Record* is that humor as it appears in the *Record*, without gestures and inflections, is terribly flat. Perusing the *Congressional Record*, one finds notations of laughter, but that does not convey the ambience of the chamber or knowledge of past verbal jousts between the participants. In an interview, I asked former senator Robert Dole (R-KS) how likely it was that humor would take place on the floor of the Senate. He answered, "possible" but that "you wouldn't find it often in the *Record*" (1997). Finally, congresspersons are allowed to revise their remarks prior to the publication of the final version of the *Record*. Senator Sam Ervin (D-NC) writes, "As my good friend Senator Paul Douglas, of Illinois, was wont to say, every speaker has three speeches: the one he intends to make, the one he actually makes, and the one he wished he had made. By permitting a representative or senator to revise his remarks as originally transcribed for its permanent edition, the *Congressional Record* allows him to make the speech he wished he had made. These considerations engender my belief that in spots the *Record* is more a work of fiction than one of fact" (1983, 141–42).

3. Matthews is not adverse to using humorous stories as material to discuss senate norms. He uses this story by Barkley, as well as at least two other humorous instances included in our data to discuss norms.

4. This alleged incident did not take place within the time parameters that I have adopted for this study. However, I include it since it is an anecdote that was submitted to Senator Wiley during the Eightieth Congress. Apparently, it had meaning for members through that time. The book by Senator Wiley is especially interesting as a source of humor. It resulted from a letter he sent to all members of the Eightieth Congress requesting that they send him their favorite humorous story. Hence it is an unusually rich cache of congressional humor circa 1946.

5. Though Huey Long was a maverick, some important members of the Senate professed a grudging respect for him. James E. Watson (R-IN), former majority leader, for example, offers this characterization of Long: "Huey was a tremendous fellow, and of course everybody was horrified when he was killed by an assassin's bullet. It was a great pity that he was so wild and untamable, and so lacking in that ability to fit in with an organization and to go along with a majority which is so essential to party coherence and, finally, to correct legislation" (1936, 306–7). And Alben Barkley also sees something of value in Long: "It was easy to disapprove of him politically, but hard to dislike him personally—though I was locked in battle with him almost constantly. One day in the cloakroom I told him, 'Huey, you are the smartest lunatic I ever saw in my whole life.' He threw back his head, laughed, and said, 'Maybe that is the smartest description I've ever had applied to me.' I went on to tell him, 'You are clever, you are resourceful, you are a great debater: if you only had a balance wheel inside you, like the little gadget in machinery, to keep you from doing so many crazy things, you would be a really great man'" (1954, 159).

6. Though it does not fall within the four decades targeted by this study, a story told by Congressman Udall is relevant: "Sometimes during these late hours one or two members will seek solace in drink. One night Senator Ted Stevens of Alaska fulminated that the Republicans were being run roughshod by the Democrats. 'There's just enough Scotch in me to demand that I get my full rights,' he roared to the bemusement of the newsmen wearily keeping the deathwatch. Later that evening, after his colleagues expressed astonishment that he would publicly confess to being drunk, Stevens hastily sought recognition to insist that he had been

referring to his Scottish heritage, *not* the amber liquid of the same name" (1988, 141, emphasis in original).

One finds more stories about drunkenness in the House than in the Senate. Watson relates this story, set in the context of a House member's making reference to a minor event that took place on June 9, 1876: "Mr. Williams and a certain other very able Democrat entered and walked down the aisle to their seats on the Democratic side, their arms around each other, weaving back and forth, holding each other up. . . . The spifflicated member solemnly asked him: 'What date did the gen'leman fixsh?' and received the answer, 'The ninth day of June.' He then sat down and the two got their heads together and buzzed a while. . . . 'I want to shay to the gen'leman,' said he, 'that the date ish entirely shatishfact'ry ,' and the two got up, put their arms around each other, and waddled back up the aisle to the cloakroom" (1936, 287).

A couple of recent Senate events involving alcoholism include the Senate's refusal to confirm one of its former members, Senator John Tower (R-TX) to be secretary of defense, and the sexual harassment case against Senator Robert Packwood (R-OR). In the latter case, Senator Packwood blamed his problems on alcoholism and entered a treatment facility, but only after newspaper stories about his sexual misconduct appeared and he faced the prospect of a Senate Ethics Committee inquiry into the allegations ("Tower Nomination Spurned by Senate" 1989; "Sen. Packwood Resigns in Disgrace" 1995).

4

Cruel Humor: The Integration of African American Members into Congress

Congress is so strange. A man gets up to speak and says nothing. Nobody listens—and then everybody disagrees.

—Boris Marshalov, Russian observer
after visiting the House of Representatives

All organizations, including those legislative, must deal with the socialization of new members. When that process involves representatives who speak for new members of the population, the process itself is put to the test. What role does humor play in the integration of new congressional members who represent previously unrepresented groups? The most severe test of this process for Congress was the admission of African Americans into the national legislature. Not only had they been unrepresented in Congress prior to the post–Civil War amendments, but they had also been politically and socially disenfranchised. During two centuries of slavery, they were considered less than human, as property to be bought and sold; they were physically abused and treated socially in ways that denigrated their essential humanity. Humor was integral to this process. It was employed by slave owners as a method of ridiculing slaves and especially as a way of denying male slaves their masculinity. If humor played a vital role in keeping African Americans in the shackles of slavery—what part did it have in their integration?

To understand humor's role in the integration of African Americans into the institution of Congress, it is helpful to view the process through the legacy of African American humor, which traces its roots to the period of slavery and before that to its African origins (Gates 1988, esp. chaps. 1

and 2). While enslaved, African Americans resorted to humor to ease their pain, to strengthen their solidarity, and to help them interpret their condition. Faced with a system of total control by plantation owners, they had to rely on their wit to survive. "Inwardly masochistic, indeed tragic, externally aggressive, even acrimonious, their humor generated several distinctive forms of expression, such as gallows humor, the ironic curse, double meanings, trickster tales, and retaliatory tales" (Boskin and Dorinson 1987, 109). Trickster humor and double meanings seemed to be especially important (Osofsky 1969, 21–23, 45–48). "Sambo," "Jim Crow," "Jim Dandy," and "Rastus" were variations of the fool and buffoon stereotypes created by whites to justify their treatment of blacks and to maintain their control over them (Boskin 1986). Indeed, even humor that blacks shared with one another at times seemed to accept the stereotypes assigned to them. Legendary black author Langston Hughes, for example, writes how some African Americans told humorous stories that related their blackness to their lack of punctuality, others accepted that blacks would always foul things up (Hughes 1966, 11–12). Daryl Dance notes that traditional tales "emphasize the role of God in explaining why Blacks are, to quote from one tale, 'so messed up,' why they are Black, why they have big, ugly feet and hands, why their hair is kinky, and why they must remain poor laborers in a rich society" (1978, 3). Dance argues, however, that in such traditional tales "the butts of the jokes are only ostensibly Blacks— the real targets are often whites or America" (5).

By the 1860s minstrel shows became popular, with whites putting on blackface and bright red lips to mimic the character of Sambo. Within a few decades blacks were putting on their own "Sambo" shows, sometimes with different contents, depending on whether the audience was white or black. Until the last half of the twentieth century, black entertainers believed that, to survive, they had to perpetuate the stereotype of Sambo before white audiences because "to laugh openly at the 'man,' 'Mr. Charley,' 'Miss Ann,' 'pig,' 'honkey,' and 'vanilla,' was to invite certain punishment" (Dorinson and Boskin 1988, 176; see also, Boskin and Dorinson 1987, 112–13). However, with the civil rights revolution of the 1950s and 1960s, the social climate changed. Such entertainers as Dick Gregory, Redd Foxx, Godfrey Cambridge, "Moms" Mabley, and Richard Pryor drew laughs by openly ridiculing the racial stereotypes that had been created and passed on to keep African Americans in their place. Through the vehicle of humor, their treatment of these stereotypes became cultural commentaries and points of racial pride (Dorinson and Boskin 1988, 177–79; Boskin and Dorinson 1987, 113–17; and Nilsen and Nilsen 2000, 15–16). It is difficult to overestimate the significance of this humor by popular black entertainers as important sources of social and political change in the nation at large.

With this rich and important heritage of African American humor as a background, it seems reasonable to suppose that black congressional members would draw on it. Be that as it may, there is not much basis to be found for this supposition in the congressional humor lore. Thus, when nine noted congressional humorists (who served between 1994 and 1998) were asked for names of other current members noted for humor, no names of African American members were suggested. Further when I searched five books dealing with congressional humor, including two by historians of the subject, I found very few of references of any kind to African American members.[1] When I searched eight books written by members of Congress that were about congressional humor or contained chapters or significant sections devoted to congressional humor, I again found a paucity of references to humor by African American members of Congress.[2] At the same time, I did not find an abundance of racial humor by Caucasian members. This by itself is of interest, given the role humor had played in portraying blacks during the slavery period. So, how can we account for this disparity?

In all, sixty-nine African Americans were elected to Congress between 1869 and 1993, the period covered by this study (Swain 1993, 20–22, 30–33). To examine congressional humor involving race, it is useful to consider that which occurred during three periods: from 1869 to 1929, from 1929 to 1964, and from 1964 to 1993. The first period covers the adoption of the post–Civil War amendments, the Reconstruction period and its crash ending with the imposition of Jim Crow laws, and the beginning migration of African Americans to Northern urban areas. The second period includes the continuing migration of blacks into Northern cities; World War II and executive order 8802, issued by President Franklin Roosevelt forbidding discrimination in defense industries; the integration of the military by President Truman; and the beginnings of the civil rights protests. The third period includes heightened racial protests; the passage of extensive civil rights, legislation including the Civil Rights Act of 1964, the Voting Rights Act of 1965, the Fair Housing Act of 1968; and the adoption of affirmative action programs. Naturally, these dates should not be considered hard and fast but approximate, since each period blends into the next. They are useful because the character of racial humor in Congress changes at about these times.

RACIAL HUMOR IN CONGRESS, 1869–1929

Much of the racial humor in Congress during the period of 1869 to 1929 comported with the "Sambo" type of humor, which was rampant in the country at large; indeed, it was not unusual to find black Americans who, as the subjects of humor, were referred to as "Sambos." Representative Samuel "Sunset" Cox (D-OH, -NY, 1857–1889) notes that although he was not impressed with the African American's skill in logical debate, nonetheless, "When a colored member makes a hit, it is reckoned the better for the social disability of the source. The retort of the African, even when feeble, is received with exhilaration, if not rapture." He quotes Dr. Johnson by saying that the marvel of dancing dogs is not that they dance well but that they dance at all. He goes on: "We have had during the past few years some half-dozen colored members. They have not, with one exception, shone aloft and alone like stars or the primal virtues. The ratiocinative is not conspicuous in their elocution, but it was compensated for by their quick susceptibility to humor" ([1880] 1969, 254–55). This latter comment suggests that black members did use humor in their legislative work during this early period. Still, not a shred of it shows up in the humor lore about Congress.

One genre of racial humor employed during this period by Southern Democrats was to accuse Republicans of using African Americans as a means to stay in office. For instance, Boykin found the following story in the *Congressional Record* in remarks made by noted congressional humorist Representative W. Jasper Talbert (D-SC), who served in the House from 1893 until 1903. Talbert told a story of an old Republican who dies and tries to get into Heaven but is told by the saints that he can't get in unless he is riding into Heaven, which he isn't.

> So the poor old Republican went away, sorrow-stricken, down the hill. At the bottom of the hill he met old black Uncle Sambo. He said to him "Where are you going?" "I'm going to Heaven," replied Uncle Sambo. "Well," said the old Republican, "you can't get in unless you ride in." "Well, what are we to do?" asked Uncle Sambo. "I will tell you, Uncle. Just let me get up on your back, and you carry me up to the gate. I will knock and they will ask me if I am riding. I will say 'yes' and then they will open the door, and I will just ride in on your back and we'll both get in that way." Uncle Sambo agreed to that and thought it would be a good idea. So the Republican got up on Uncle Sambo's shoulders and went back to the gate of Heaven. He knocked and the saint came and opened the door again and said, "Who is there?" The Republican told him. "Are you riding?" asked the saint. "Yes," replied the old Republican. "Well, just hitch your horse outside and come right in." . . . That's just the way you're doing. You still want to ride into office on the back of Uncle Sambo. When you get there, you get in and he has to be hitched outside like a mule. (Boykin 1961, 9–10)

Another story in which Democrats accuse Republicans of using African Americans was told by Senator Roger Q. Mills (D-TX) during a tariff debate in 1894:

That reminds me of a story I heard in Texas of a man who said he had fallen asleep. He had a dream and he dreamed he went to hell. He was telling about what he saw when he got down there, and some fellow, who was a politician, asked him, "Did you see any Democrats down there?" He said, "Oh, yes; there were a few, not many, but there were a few around." "What were they doing?" "They were talking about reducing taxation and things of that sort, trying to do something for the public good." "Did you see any Populists down there?" "Yes, there were a few Populists." "What were they talking about?" "They were talking about having a good time in hell by issuing greenback money, $150 for every individual in hell." "Did you see any Republicans down there?" "Oh, yes." "What were they doing?" "Every one of them was holding a Negro between them and the fire." (Boykin 1961, 303)

As one might expect from the foregoing, some stories from this period portray African Americans as ignorant. These stories are typically spiced up by one's telling them in the dialect of the poor and uneducated. Common references include "an old colored man," an "old colored preacher," or "uncle." Generally, the racism in the humor is more blatant and demeaning than that in later periods. One such tale was told by "Private" John Allen (D-MS), who served in the House of Representatives at the end of the nineteenth century and who Champ Clark hailed as one of the half-dozen best humorists ever to serve in the House (1920, 185). "In my first campaign an old colored man came up to greet me after the meeting. 'Marse Allen,' he said, 'I'se powerful glad to see you. I'se known ob you sense you was a baby. Knew yoh pappy long befo' you-all was bohn, too. He used to hold de same office fo' years an' years.' 'What office do you mean, uncle?' I asked, as I never knew pop held any office. 'Why de office ob candidate, Marse John; yoh pappy was candidate fo' many years'" (Wiley 1947, 34–35). Another was told by W. Jasper Talbert in addressing the tedium of silver speeches during the 1890s: "Mr. Speaker, in thinking about this much discussed subject, my mind reverts back to the old Negro preacher who was addressing his flock with great earnestness on the subject of miracles. He said, 'My beloved friends and brethren, the greatest of all miracles was 'bout de loves and de fishes. There was five thousand loaves and two thousand fishes, and de twelve apostles had to eat 'em all. Now the miracle is that they didn't bust.' Now the people, Mr. Speaker, have been stuffed on this subject for the last three weeks, or, I might say, for the last few years, with silver speeches, and the great wonder is that they haven't 'busted'" (Boykin 1961, 337). Yet another story, this one unintentionally humorous and the funnier for it, involves Congressman Ben Butler (R-MA), who was known as a stout champion of civil rights during the Gilded Age. He "arranged for his son, a West Point graduate, to serve for a time with a regiment of blacks on the Western Plains. And when the first black Congressman met with a cold reception on his arrival in Washington, Butler went out of his way to make him feel at home in the House. His concern for blacks was so great that when he went to Richmond to deliver an address to a black convention, the master of ceremonies, a black preacher, introduced him with the words, 'General Butler may have a white face, but he has a black heart'" (Boller 1991, 150).

Champ Clark, in his book *My Quarter Century of American Politics*, includes a couple of humorous stories involving race that might be called "escape" humor. In each case, the politicians need to use their wits to extricate themselves from political and possibly even personal danger regarding the race question. The first case involves the wily Tom Corwin (W-R-OH). At a time when abolitionist sentiment was reaching a fever pitch, the naturally dark complexioned Corwin found himself confronted with a cleverly laid trap by a member of the audience at a campaign rally.

Are you in favor of a law permitting colored people to eat at the same tables with white folks, in hotels and on steamboats? "Black Tom" did not follow the Scriptural injunction, "Let your communication be yea, yea; nay, nay." That was too concise and direct for the end he had in view, which was to dodge, or, in prize-ring parlance, to "duck." If he should answer "Yea," all the pro-slavery votes would be cast against him and he would be defeated. Should he answer "Nay" the Abolitionists would defeat him. He answered neither "Yea" nor "Nay," but—his dark mobile countenance shining with the gladness of certain victory—he replied: "Fellow citizens, I submit that it is improper to ask that question of a gentleman of my color!" The crowd delirious with delight, yelled itself hoarse, and the "Wagon-Boy" carried the day and the election. (Clark 1920, 187–88)

The second example of escape humor involves Senator Edward O. Wolcott (R-CO), who served in the Senate from 1889 until 1901. A great public speaker, he was sent into the South to espouse Republicanism.

At a certain place, he was politely informed that the "rally" would begin and end at the same time, and that not since 1883 had any Republican been permitted to finish a speech there. Wolcott was determined, however, and, upon learning that the citizens, as a rule, were kind enough to permit speakers to get out of town and fill their next appointment, he concluded to make his speech as billed. . . . Wolcott began his speech at once, with one of his best stories. The audience was separated, with the colored folk all being in the gallery and only white people below. In about five minutes Wolcott's discretion was overcome by his Republicanism, and he made a pointed thrust at the opponent party, whereupon a body of young men in the center of the theater shouted in concert, "Rats!" Wolcott paused for a moment, and then, waving his hand at the gallery, said, "Waiter, come down and take the Chinamen's orders!" The effect was electrical and effectual. In laughingly referring to the incident afterward the Senator said, "You should have seen that dusky hillside of faces in the gallery break into ledges of pearl." (Clark 1920, 194–95)

All together, the image that emerges of African Americans in the congressional humor lore of this early period is that of Sambo. During this time, African Americans were presented as ignorant and illiterate, albeit happy. They had no will of their own but existed to be used by others; they did not cause things to happen—things happened to them. It would not be too strong to say they were portrayed as buffoon characters. References to blacks in congressional stories are insulting by contemporary standards, though we find no vicious racial attacks. However, in characterizing the racial utterances of Caucasian members, we must keep in mind that when looking at the public humor of congresspersons, we are studying the public communication behavior of an elite population that might be quite different from the humor of the masses or from the private humor of the elites. That is, congressional members might avoid racial epitaphs in public discourse, yet they may liberally sprinkle their private speech with the worst of the worst.

It is noteworthy that none of the humor books or member biographies I examined contained any humor by or about African American members who served in Congress during this period, save a lone reference by Sam Cox. Part of this result may be attributable to the number of African Americans who served in Congress during the period between 1869 and 1929. A total of twenty-two were elected during this time; all were from Southern states, and all were Republicans. Between 1891 and 1901 there was no more than one black member of Congress at any one time, and there were no African American members between 1901 and 1929 (Swain 1993, 20–22, 30–33). However, the smallness of numbers alone cannot account for this outcome. If humor is a social activity, as is often contended, it is as though these members were nonpersons. The lore simply does not take cognizance of their presence.

RACIAL HUMOR OF CAUCASIAN
MEMBERS OF CONGRESS 1929–1964

As found in the congressional humor literature after 1929, Caucasian members of Congress made a perceptible shift in the nature of their racial humor. Specifically, the public congressional humor involving race now saw a lessening of meanness when contrasted to the racial humor of the earlier period, with its "Sambo" stories and with its characterization of blacks as tools of Republicans; likewise, the shift is also in contrast to the stories passed informally between segregationist-minded members of Congress (see, e.g., Parker 1986, esp. 71–72). In general, there were no crude references to racial characteristics. However, most of the stories involving race were still in the dialect of uneducated blacks and still included references to an "old colored man," "uncle," a "Negro preacher," or a "colored boy." These seem demeaning to us now but were probably taken as an improvement by contemporaries. While the dialect of the poor and uneducated was the norm for these stories, the punch lines often revealed a strong native intelligence of the poor African Americans who "upped" upper-class white elites.

An example of this kind of story was told by Senator Reed Smoot (R-UT, 1903–1933) about a contemporary of his whom Reed characterized "as a very pompous man who was over-impressed with his own importance." "One day he was being shaved by an old colored barber in one of the Washington hotels, a man who had seen many Senators come and go. The Senator remarked to the barber, 'Uncle,' you must have had among your customers many of my distinguished predecessors in the Senate?' 'Yes, sar,' answered the barber, 'I'se knowed most of dem; by de way, you remind me of Dan'l Webster.' The gratified statesman, placing his finger to his forehead, said, 'Is is my brow or my speeches?' 'No boss, 'it's your breath'" (Wiley 1947, 21).

Congressman Luther A. Johnson (D-TX), who served from 1923 to 1946, sent Senator Alexander Wiley[3] a story about Johnson's time as a county prosecutor—in particular, right after he had just completed his case against the defendant and was built up and let down by a young African American boy.

> The weather was exceedingly warm, and as I was leaving the Courthouse after finishing my speech, I met a colored boy, aged about fourteen years, who worked at the hotel where I was stopping, and, addressing me, he said, "Mr. Luther, that sure was a good speech you just made." I began fumbling in my pocket, trying to locate a dime to pay him for the compliment, but before I could locate a dime, he said again, "Mr. Luther, I believe that was the best speech I ever heard." I then commenced trying to locate a quarter, thinking a compliment of that kind was worth at least that amount, but before I could do so, he said again, "Mr. Luther, tell me, was you trying to put him in or get him out?" Needless to say, he didn't get the quarter or any other tip. (Wiley 1947, 54–55)

A similar story was told by Senator Alben Barkley in his biography, when he was discussing his views on prohibition. "I never think of this lady's summation of my position without being reminded of the old Negro well digger who worked for a devout Methodist lady. One day he collapsed while digging, and she revived him with a few drops of medicinal spirits, which might as well have been administered with an eye dropper. When he came to, he remarked, 'You know, Miz Cole is a fine lady. But she is so afraid she might do wrong, she afraid to do what's right!'" (Barkley 1954, 42).

Sometimes these "upmanship" stories spoof the congressperson's position of importance. One such story was told to Senator Wiley by Representative James Mead (D-NY): "A member of the clergy rang the bell of a colonial mansion and Eph, an equally aged colored servant, answered the door. The minister, seeking contributions to his church asked, 'Is the master of the house a Christian?' 'Nossuh, Nossuh,' said the old Negro emphatically. 'He am a member of Congress'" (Wiley 1947, 11; see also the story submitted to Wiley by both Senators Fulbright and Gillette discussed in chapter 3, p. 53).

Despite a tendency for the racial stories in congressional humor during the 1930s and 1940s to be more civil and respectful than those in the earlier period, several nonetheless still portray African Americans as ignorant and shiftless. A story about a shiftless black man was told by Congressman J. Hardin Peterson (D-FL), who served from 1933 to 1951. "An old colored man was brought to court because he was behind in his alimony payments. The Judge said, 'Josh, you told me you'd pay Liza $3 a week when I gave you the divorce and now you are only paying her $1.50. What's the trouble?' Josh said, 'Jedge, when I quit Liza to marry Mary I thought Mary was a better worker, but she ain't making as much money as I thought she would'" (Wiley 1947, 154). One that reflected the putative ignorance of African Americans was offered by Senator C. Douglas Buck (R-DE), who served from 1943 to 1949. "When I was Governor of Delaware, I drove to a distant town in a car bearing the official license. Arriving at my destination, I pulled up in front a hotel and a small colored bellboy, who had seen me drive in, walked up to get my bag. As he started back to the hotel, he asked, 'Mistah, is you the Gov'nah?' I replied that I was. After taking a few more steps, he said, 'Mistah, I means is you the Gov'nah hisself?' I said, 'Yes, I am the Governor.' As I looked at him, his face broke into a broad smile, and he said, 'Youse the first one of dem things I've evah see'd'" (Wiley 1947, 222).[4]

As indicated, blacks are portrayed more civilly during this period in congressional humor stories, though these stories are usually still in dialect and in the language of the poor and uneducated. I cannot account for this change in the tenor of congressional humor by an increase in the number of African American in Congress. In point of fact, during this time the number shrunk drastically. Between 1929 and 1945, roughly the first half of this period, there were only three black members of Congress, only one in any given year. All were from Illinois. In total there were only seven black members of Congress during this entire period; all but one were Democrats, and, in contrast to the earlier period, none were from the South. No, the change of treatment is more likely due to the migration of blacks to the industrial North; to the organization and activities of organizations such as the NAACP; and to the changing public attitudes about race, a process that undoubtedly accelerated with World War II and its aftermath.

Adam Clayton Powell: Trickster in Congress

The controversial Congressman from Harlem, Adam Clayton Powell, is the only African American member who is referenced in congressional humor sources for the period 1929 to 1964. Interestingly, many of the stories about him that are included in these sources were taken directly from his biography, *Adam by Adam* ([1971] 1994).

Shortly after Powell arrived in Washington to serve in Congress, he met with Speaker of the House Sam Rayburn. Rayburn commented, "'Adam, everyone down here expects you to come with a bomb in both hands. Now don't do that. Oh, I know all about you and I know that you can't be quiet very long, but don't throw those bombs. Just see how things operate here. Take your time. Freshmen members of Congress are supposed not to be heard and not even to be seen too much.' . . . I said, 'Mr. Speaker, I've got a bomb in each hand and I'm going to throw them right away.' He almost died laughing" (71–72; see also Boller 1991, 61). Apparently the two men got along fine after this icebreaker.

In another story about Powell, also related in Boller, Powell is the target of humor in a story that he seems to relish. Just prior to the 1960 Democratic Convention, Congressman Hale Boggs (D-LA) was presiding over an informal discussion about persons who might be considered eligible for the party's nomination that year. Names that came up were Jack Kennedy, Stuart Symington, and Hubert Humphrey. One by one they were dismissed. Kennedy was a Catholic; Symington was too stiff and couldn't project himself; and Humphrey talked too much. "Then, Boggs, just for fun, said, 'Well, now, what about Adam Clayton Powell?' The group of Southern Democrats was speechless, and before anyone could answer, Boggs said, 'Your right. The country's not ready for a Baptist preacher to be President!'" (217; see also Boller 1991, 62).

When Powell came to Congress in 1945, there was only one other black member of Congress, William A. Dawson (D-IL). They both came from safe urban black districts, but any further similarity between them ends there. Political scientist James Q. Wilson contrasts their styles in an article that appeared in 1960.

When Dawson arrived in Washington in 1943 to begin his first term in the House, the House restaurant and barbershop as well as other member facilities were segregated. He and his staff did nothing to challenge these arrangements. He consciously shunned race issues, though he did vote in favor of bills that would improve the economic condition of his constituents. His apprehension about racially divisive issues was so great that at the 1952 Democratic Convention he used his seat on the platform committee to argue for a watered-down civil rights plank rather than the stronger one that party liberals favored (Hamilton 1991, 197; Powell

[1971] 1994, 90–91). However, Dawson was also known for his quiet work behind the scenes, his steadiness, and his dependability. He behaved like a House insider and was widely respected not only for the manner in which he chaired the House Government Operations Committee but also for how he conducted himself in personal matters. In effect, he increased his effectiveness within the institution as well as his ability to bring patronage to his constituents by treading lightly where race issues were concerned (Wilson 1960, esp. 355–61).

Congressman Powell was as different from Dawson as night is from day. He was personally flamboyant, even arrogant, and he raised the issue of racial injustice at every opportunity. He deliberately set out to be "a congressional irritant" and held the appellation of "Mr. Civil Rights" among fellow African Americans—that is, until his own questionable behavior itself became the issue. He dined in the congressional restaurant, used other congressional facilities, and introduced a resolution providing that African Americans employed in the Capitol be admitted to the Capitol cafeteria. He also advocated that black federal employees eat in dining facilities provided for federal employee use. When he saw there were no black journalists using the congressional press galleries, he demanded that they become integrated. He authored the Powell amendment, which provided that federal money could not be spent to support segregated facilities, and he introduced it time after time. He endorsed President Eisenhower rather than Adlai Stevenson in the election of 1956, after he found he could work with the Republican administration to end segregation in the executive branch of government (Hamilton 1991, 482–84; Powell [1971] 1994, 70–84). He frequently held press conferences and enjoyed the publicity as well as the banter with members of the press. He became chair of the House Education and Labor Committee during the 1960s, only to be stripped of his seniority, his chairmanship, and even his seat in the House. (In a special election that followed, Harlemites returned him to Congress by a seven-to-one majority.) He was erratic. Other civil rights leaders, as well as officials in the Johnson administration, found Powell to be unreliable, sometimes even devious (Hamilton 1991, 446, 466, 484–85; Hickey and Edwin 1965, 8–9). His fecklessness was never more evident than during the fight to enact the 1964 Civil Rights Act: when others were going sleepless to enact this landmark legislation, Powell was deep-sea fishing in the Bahamas (Udall 1988, 111). Forced to defend his misuse of committee funds and his questionable European travel, he defiantly asserted, "I wish to state emphatically that I will always do just what every other Congressman and committee chairman has done, is doing and will do" (Hamilton 1991, 409). In short, he was the equal of every other member, even in abusing his public position. Andrew Young was moved to quip, "Rosa Parks integrated buses, James Meredith integrated the University of

Mississippi, Martin Luther King, Jr., integrated churches and lunch counters. But it was left to Adam Clayton Powell to integrate corruption" (Udall 1988, 116).

On the record Congressman Powell spoke forthrightly and with gravity to the substance of issues. His constituents supported him because he was not afraid to tell white folks things his constituents felt themselves; he was unique among federal public officials in his time for his courage in this respect. He was not known for telling humorous stories; rather than make witty remarks, use word play, and create clever incongruities of thought to reach out to other members, his humor was caustic. Some of his actions and offhanded comments fit quite well into a type of humor known as "trickster" humor, which can be traced back to American slavery origins.[5] In this kind of humor, the slave outwardly accepts his lot and shows respect for his master, but in private he vents his real feelings and, in stories, perhaps apocryphal, regularly outsmarts his master. This humor often stems from double meanings and demonstrates a playfulness and deception. At times the trickster would lie and steal from the "massa" as a way of improving his lot, and, at other times, he would do so for reasons of survival (see Cowan 2001; and Levine 1977, 102–33, 370–86).

The "John-Massa" stories in particular illustrate trickster humor (though we could also use Brer Rabbit stories). In one such story, "John cusses out his massa whenever he pleases—whenever the massa is up at the big house and John is down in the field. John steals food and lies his way out of trouble by changing a pig into a baby and, when caught, reverses the magic" (Dorinson and Boskin 1988, 174). In another, "John has a passion for onions and busily steals them from his master's garden each night. When the master suspects there is a thief around, he asks John to catch him. John returns with the culprit, a skunk, and tells his master if he doesn't believe the varmint was the crook, 'he could smell the skunk's breath himself'" (Osofsky 1969, 46–47). Another story has the master eating "high on the hog" while his slaves went hungry. Strangely, one day some of the massa's hogs died of "malitis." Rather than feed the suspicious critters to his family, massa ordered them fed to the slaves. "What was the mysterious plague? A former bondsman described it this way: 'One of the strongest Negroes got up early in the morning, long 'fore the rising horn called the slaves from their cabins. He skitted to the hog pen with a heavy mallet in his hand. When he tapped Mister Hog 'tween the eyes with that mallet, 'malitis' set in mighty quick" (Osofsky 1969, 47, quoting Botkin 1944). In a story that illustrates the importance of double meanings, a slave named Faithful Jack pays homage to his master, who is on his deathbed. As the master dies, the slave says, "Farewell, massa! Pleasant Journey! You soon be dere, massa—[it's] all de way down hill!" (Osofsky 1969, 23). Levine writes that "the trickster and the need for the trickster, endured long past slavery" (1977, 347). According to him, most slavery trickster stories continued to be told in several versions well into the twentieth century (371).

Several stories can be used to illustrate Congressman Powell's actions as a trickster. A stalwart champion of segregation, Congressman John E. Rankin (D-MS) issued a statement that Powell's election was a disgrace and that he would not let Powell sit by him. Powell retaliated by making it a point to do just that. "Whenever Rankin entered the Chamber, I followed after him, sitting as close to him as I could. One day the press reported that he moved five times" (A. C. Powell [1971] 1994, 73). The fastidious Senator John McClellan (D-AR), defender of segregation, would squirm when Powell admonished him to "keep the faith, baby"; other times, Powell would smile and address the senator by his first name, "See you later, John," while the senator's face would burn red (Parker 1986, 56, 58). When the most outspoken racist in the Senate, Theodore Bilbo (D-MS), commented that there was one good Negro in Congress but that Powell was a bad Negro because he continued to use congressional facilities not meant for "Negroes," Powell gamely entitled one of the chapters in his autobiography, "First Bad Nigger in Congress" ([1971] 1994, 70–84).

Secretary of the Navy James V. Forestal, whom Powell characterizes as "one of the grandest men who ever breathed," figured in a trickster incident staged by Powell, this one involving willful deceit. The congressman was determined to appoint a highly qualified African American to the Annapolis Naval Academy since no black had ever gotten beyond the first year in the long history of that institution. He consulted an educator in the District of Columbia and came up with the name of an African American with an outstanding record, Wesley Brown, who on Powell's recommendation was appointed to Annapolis. After a few months, Powell wrote a letter to Forrestal complaining that Brown was about to be put out of the academy. Concerned, Forrestal went to Annapolis to inquire, only to find that the midshipman was doing very well and so informed Powell in a letter. Powell was not surprised since he had totally fabricated the letter about Brown's poor treatment. Sometime later Powell ran into Forrestal at a cocktail party. "'Adam,' said Forrestal, 'why did you lie to me?' 'Jim,' said Powell, 'I had to lie in order to make sure that Wesley Brown would not be touched by anyone'" ([1971] 1994, 78–79; see also Boller 1991, 62).

While a member of Congress, Powell lived lavishly. He cut the figure of a high-living, fun-loving, woman-chasing playboy. He was very handsome; he owned several homes and two boats; he dressed nattily; he was frequently seen in some of the most exclusive night clubs; and he drove a sporty Jaguar convertible around the capital—this while representing a district in which most citizens were extremely poor. Yet, he didn't fear electoral reprisals. "His manner of living and his obvious pleasure in moving freely in the white man's world contrast sharply with the slum life of the average Negro, especially those in Harlem. He has plumbed deeper than any other Negro leader the vicarious sense of many lower-class Negroes. 'When my people see a picture of me in '21,' says Powell, 'or some other downtown night club, they like it. They know I can pass for white, but that I'm as black in my thinking as the blackest of them'" (Hickey and Edwin 1965, 2; see also Wilson 1960, 354–55).[6] Robert Parker, an African American and LBJ's long-time chauffeur who later served as headwaiter of the Senate Dining Room, recalls another instance involving Powell in which the black waiters in an upscale night spot took satisfaction from Powell's high living ways.

> The third floor elevator door slid open (at Harvey's, a restaurant influential Washington politicians often frequented) and there he stood in a three piece suit, a cigar clenched in his white teeth. On each arm was a beautiful white woman. . . . He sat at a table near two southern senators. "If you were down in my part of the country," one of them said loud enough for everyone to hear, "you'd get strung up." "I can"t understand why," Powell shot back. "You white cats have been doing what you please with our black woman for as long as you wanted." The senators forced a laugh, but they never forgot the "insult." Neither did the waiters. We felt as if Powell had put those senators in their place just for us. (Parker 1986, 59)

Representative Morris Udall recounts the impressions of a colleague, a member of Powell's committee, who visited Powell in his congressional office.

> Arriving at the door, the congressman was greeted by a buxom receptionist, who escorted him past a number of stunning secretaries into the chairman's private office, which was carpeted with an exquisite Persian rug Powell had purchased on a junket to the Middle East. Embracing the junior member, Powell proffered an expensive Havana cigar he had just brought back from Cuba. He then sauntered to an antique sideboard groaning under a collection of exquisite French wines and Spanish sherries brought back from another "investigative" trip to Paris, and poured two glasses of port. Taking in the splendor, the younger man said, "Mr. Chairman, you really go first cabin." Powell grinned and said, "Yes, these are the fruits of serving Jesus." (Udall 1988, 110)

Powell knew the race game and played it skillfully. As Parker notes, Powell "was light-skinned for a black man, and he used it to his advantage. Many white congressmen, for example, believed that the lighter the Negro, the smarter he was, and Powell did nothing to dissuade them" (1986, 56). But true to his trickster nature, Hickey and Edwin offer this picture: "'Adam views himself as a joke on the whole white race,' one of Powell's closest allies from the past has said. 'They think he's a Negro.

And he views himself as a joke on all Negroes. They think he's a Negro too'" (Hickey and Edwin 1965, 15; the aid who is quoted is not identified). In a congressional debate, Powell once admonished, "Beware of Greeks bearing gifts, colored men looking for loans, and whites who understand the Negro" (Udall 1988, 110). And in another instance, Udall recalls, "When another member proposed a vaguely worded amendment, Powell was dubious. 'I'm not sure what this means,' he said. 'I suspect a Caucasian in the woodpile'" (Udall 1988, 110).

CONGRESSIONAL HUMOR RELATING TO RACE, 1964–1993

Between 1964 and 1993, forty African Americans were elected to Congress, all but one to the House of Representatives. The lone Senator was Edward Brooke of Massachusetts, and he was also the only black Republican to serve during this period. Most of them came from states outside the South. Regardless of their regional origin, the African American membership that served during this period included some very strong and talented persons who took an active part in the public discourse of Congress.

The congressional humor lore beginning around 1964 changed to reflect what was transpiring in the nation at large regarding race relations. The congressional humor books and the books written by congresspersons included in this study that were published after the passage of the 1964 Civil Rights Act do not contain stories with references such as "old Negro," "young colored boy," or "uncle." Moreover, the dialect of the poor, uneducated African American is not used to tell stories about black people. In prior periods, so far as congressional humor lore is concerned, it was as though there had been no African Americans in Congress, with the exception of Adam Clayton Powell. Beginning with this period, we find stories told in the first person by African American members such as Representatives Barbara Jordan and John Conyers, and we find some witty remarks of Representatives Adam Clayton Powell and Ron Dellums. The humor by and about African Americans in the congressional humor lore during this period is much like that of Caucasian members, drawing on sarcasm, ridicule, self-effacing humor, and so on. However, the literature does not have the great quantity of humor by black members as it does by that of white members.

Congresswoman Barbara Jordan (D-TX) is the only African American member of Congress who was referenced in more than one book for her humor during this period. In an anecdote appearing in Paul Boller's work (1991), we find her listening to a presentation regarding the price of fertilizer. "Once a Congressman was talking at length to the Texas delegation about the high price of fertilizer. After listening to him for a time Barbara

Jordan . . . got tired of his long-windedness. 'Congressman,' she finally said, 'it's refreshing to hear you talking about something that you're deep into'" (175; see also, Haskins 1977, 185). Another story told by Jordan, which shows her considerable ability to create humor, is included in the book on congressional humor by Angele de T. Gingras (1973). In this case, Jordan was appearing as a new member of Congress before the Washington Press Club and was asked the question, "What happened when John Connally [former Democratic governor of Texas and Nixon's secretary of the treasury] and his people reached the Jordan river?" She responded,

> They stopped. The water was black you know and somewhat treacherous. John pondered whether it would be safer to cross party lines than the Jordan.
>
> John considered the river. He asked a henchman how much it would cost to divert that little old stream to his ranch near San Antonio. But, then, who wants a river named Jordan on a Connally Ranch?
>
> A new idea flashed through his mind, his first new thought since the new economic policy. "We'll change the name of the blasted stream. We'll call it Big John. Big John? BJ? Not on your life!! Illiterate Texans would think it stood for Barbara Jordan."
>
> A second idea fought its way to his awareness. "We'll buy the river and set up a Holy water franchise. We'll bottle it for Episcopalians and sell it by the tank to Baptists."
>
> The only problem with this is the name of the blasted stream.
>
> He finally said, "What the hell, let's grab a limousine and go back to the Hilton. A camel driver will show us the way."
>
> Guess what was the name of the hotel? . . . The Jordan Hilton. (Gingras 1973, 109–10)

A reference to Congressman Ronald V. Dellums (D-CA) appears in Boller's work and relates to Dellums's objection of the use of the word "black" by the Pentagon to describe secret programs and budgets.

> They were called "black programs" or "black budgets" and Pentagon people often talked about "operations in the black world." Dellums, who was black, said he had a hard time explaining to constituents who were unfamiliar with Pentagon jargon why he had voted against this "black program" or that "black budget." So he set out to change the terminology and appeared to have succeeded, at least in part. At a meeting of the House Armed Services Committee's Research and Development Subcommittee, of which he is the new chairman, Dellums persuaded his colleagues to drop the word "black," when applied to secret programs. The term now would be "special access programs" or "special access budgets." (1991, 318–19)

Finally, Gingras includes a story told by John Conyers (D-MI). In it, the congressman returns to Detroit to the house in which he lived as a child, in the "Black Bottom" neighbohood. While having his picture taken in front of the rickety structure, a crowd gathers and begins asking questions: "Didn't you used to hang around the drugstore on the corner?" "Didn't you and your brother used to play baseball in the summer leagues?" "And didn't you used to live in this house?" Then, one man eventually says, "I know who you are. You are John Conyers. . . . Hey gang, this is John Conyers. . . . Yes, he used to live there. . . . Hey what are you doing these days?" According to Conyers, "I pulled myself together with all the aplomb of a future member of Congress, and I said—well, I'll be modest about this—and I said, 'Well, I am a Federal employee. I work for the government.' He said, 'No kidding? You're in the Post Office, too, hey'" (Gingras 1973, 97–99).

AFRICAN AMERICANS, HUMOR, AND CONGRESS

The humor among black members of Congress was high quality, but what is striking is the meager amount of it. Given the backdrop of a rich tapestry of African American humor, why isn't there more of it from the sixty-nine African American congresspersons who served between 1869 and 1993? And given the viciousness of humor regarding black Americans, why was there not more of this kind of humor addressed to African American members by Caucasian members? Equally of interest, why were black members of Congress almost totally absent from the congressional humor lore, especially until the last period?

In seeking answers to these questions, it is important to reiterate that when we study congressional humor, we are studying the humor of political elites, not that of ordinary people. For example, although we do not find an abundance of racial humor by Caucasian members of Congress, we must keep in mind that their public humor might be quite different from their private racial humor. That is, congresspersons might have avoided racial epitaphs in public discourse, yet they may have spoken at liberty during their private speech. And again, we can expect the humor of elites to be more circumspect than what we might find in the harsher, whispered, mass culture.

One possible explanation for the lack of representation of humor from African American members of Congress in the congressional humor lore is that humor is a socially shared art form and that black congresspersons were considered to be social outsiders. Plausible enough. Another possible explanation for their lack of humor takes into account black members' position in Congress and their assessment as to how they might be most effective—specifically, why being humorous probably did not figure into that strategy.

Much of the rich heritage of humor by African Americans was created in reaction to slavery, its aftermath, and the stereotyping of blacks by whites. For blacks, humor was aimed at helping them understand their low position in America and, as often it was ironic, to affirm their racial worth in the face of harsh treatment by whites. But most important, it was a humor of the masses, and it was a kind of vulnerability humor. From this perspective, it was a humor of weakness and one not appropriate for black elites who wanted to project an image of strength in the national legislature. As with white members, they might have enjoyed this humor of the masses and drawn on it abundantly in their private communication; however, they may not have found it useful in public speech.

The stereotyping by whites, and the humor that was part of it, was cruel, easily fitting into the superiority approach to humor. In his book *Sambo* (1986), Joseph Boskin discusses the dominance and control aspect built into the Sambo icon of American culture.

> Sambo was an extraordinary type of social control, at once extremely subtle, devious, and encompassing. To exercise a high degree of control meant also to be able to manipulate the full range of humor; to create, ultimately, an insidious type of buffoon. To make the black male into an object of laughter, and conversely, to force him to devise laughter, was to strip him of masculinity, dignity, and self-possession. Sambo was, then, an illustration of humor as a device of oppression, and one of the most potent in American culture. The ultimate objective of whites was to effect mastery: to render the black male powerless as a potential warrior, as a sexual competitor, and as an economic adversary. (13–14)

Elsewhere, Boskin vividly illustrates the features of this American buffoon.

> Sambo took form in popular culture as the national court-jester: slow-witted, loosely shuffling, buttock-scratching, benignly-optimistic, superstitiously-frightened, childishly-lazy, irresponsibly-carefree, rhythmically-gated, pretentiously intelligent, sexually animated. His physical characteristics added to the jester's appearance: toothy-grinned, thick-lipped, happy-haired, slack-jawed, round-eyed. The analogy ends here, however. Unlike the jester found in other cultures, Sambo was usually denied wisdom. His role before the national audience was a limited one. He served either as a comic performer or as a buffoon. (1971, 649)

African American members of Congress had to consider this pervasive and cruel tyranny of stereotypes about black people when deciding how they could be most effective in their congressional activities. How could they use humor? The dominant element of society had systematically used this humor to try to humiliate and control them and their kind. Utilizing this line of humor to tell stories and jokes was not an option for them, because to do so would be to risk playing into the Sambo/buffoon stereotype. If they allowed themselves to be defined in this framework, how could they and their ideas be taken seriously? Furthermore, they could not draw publicly on their own adaptations of that humor born of repression, vulnerability humor—that is, tricksterism, double entendres, irony, and so on. How would using it help them project an image of strength? At the same time, to attempt self-deprecating humor might mean being taken at face value and cause them to be judged as less than powerful political personalities. Thus, avoiding public humor altogether and presenting a public image of seriousness seemed to be the best choice for these members. For them, any attempt at public humor was likely to be out of the question.

The exception to this rule was the congressman from Harlem. Given the time in which Powell served, he saw no hope of reaching out to build legislative coalitions to pass civil rights legislation. Thus, he resolved to be a "congressional irritant," and what became well-suited for his purposes were trickster humor, rooted as it was in slavery humor, and acerbic humor with double meanings. His humor was not the sort to be shared with a trusted circle of colleagues. It bristled, and it was intended to call attention to the plight of black Americans. As well, he believed that he could further his cause by behaving in a way that demonstrated how, as a human being and as a congressman, he was the equal of all others in every respect, even in abusing the privileges of office.

What of the Caucasian members of Congress and their use of humor regarding African Americans? We found almost no use of the "N" word or any other comparably derogatory forms of address employed in any period in white congresspersons' public humor involving African Americans. However, during the 1869–1929 period we do find stories about "Uncle Sambo," "an old colored preacher," "a colored boy"; and racial stories were almost invariably told in the dialect of the poor and uneducated African Americans of the time. Some of the humor in the early period portrays the African Americans as simply tools of the Republican Party.

By the 1929–1964 period, a noticeable change in the structure of congressional humor about African Americans had taken place. Many of the stories feature dignified, educated elite white senators' and representatives' being "upped," or outsmarted, by the ostensibly low, illiterate black constituents. In some cases, the target of uneducated African Americans in these tales is the institution of Congress itself. However, there are still some stories about ignorant, shiftless, and poorly educated blacks, and most of the race-relevant stories regardless of structure were told in dialect. Still, the shift seems meaningful, and it might have reflected the nationalization of the race question, what with the Northern migration of blacks brought on by the two World Wars and the Great Depression. And of course, this period also saw the development of television and growing American internationalism. It was embarrassing to have America's race problems projected on screens the world over.

Guilt of the sort discussed by Swedish sociologist Gunnar Myrdal might also have played a role in changing racial attitudes. Members of Congress were elite members of society and as such were keepers of American democratic values. Myrdal, in his classic study of race relations in America (published in 1944), articulated their dilemma. On the one hand, there is what he calls the "American Creed," which consisted of ideals enshrined in the Declaration of Independence, the preamble to the Constitution, the Bill of Rights, and the several state constitutions. "These ideals of the essential dignity of the individual human being, of the fundamental equality of all men, and of certain inalienable rights to freedom, justice, and a fair opportunity represent to the American people the essential meaning of the nation's early struggle for independence" (4). On the other hand, segregation was embedded in the law of the land. The dilemma he saw was the contradiction between the values that comprise the American Creed and the festering guilt caused by the American treatment of African Americans under a system of segregation. "The American Creed represents the national conscience. The Negro is a 'problem' to the average American partly because of a palpable conflict between the status actually awarded him and those ideals" (23). As keepers of the creed, it would have been unseemly for congressional elites to publically ridicule, through uncharitable and crude humor, any segment of the American population, especially those least able to defend themselves. Add to this the fact that Myrdal discovered, to his surprise, that African Americans, like whites, were under the spell of the creed (4); it would have been downright unwise for Caucasian political elites to be a part of any humor that systematically and publicly demeaned African Americans.[7]

In no instance during the 1869–1929 period did we see the humor of an African American member of Congress cited by authors of congressional humor books or in the works of Caucasian members of Congress who were noted humorists; and, save Adam Clayton Powell, the same can be said of the period from 1929–1964. Moreover, the instances of Powell's humor that appear in a congressional humor book are taken from his biography and only appear in one of these sources that was published as late as 1991 (Boller, 60–62). Examples of his witty remarks are cited in only one of our works of congressionpersons noted for humor, this published in 1988 (Udall, 105–18).

It is only with the final period that humorous stories told by African American members of Congress appear in the literature of congressional humor. Though this seems to be a significant development, given that forty-five of the sixty-nine African American members who served in Congress through 1993 served during this period, it is their scant representation in the congressional humor literature, even at this late date, that is striking. Consider this in the light of the rich legacy of African American humor, and it only calls attention to the modest amount of humor attributed to black members and thus puts into focus the dilemma they faced.

Communication is critical to the effectiveness of individuals and groups in an institution such as Congress, and humor is an important kind of communication. Perhaps it can be suggested that the full integration of African American members into the institution of Congress will be achieved only when they feel as free as Caucasian members to draw on humor in carrying out their congressional tasks, whether it be a distinctly African American humor or a general humor, and when neither they nor their colleagues will think the better of it. It, too, will be the shared humor of community and institutional solidarity.

NOTES

1. The books by historians are by Paul Boller (1991) and Edward Boykin (1961), while the joke books are by Angele de T. Gingras (1973), Bill Hogan and Mike Hill (1987), and Alexander Wiley (1947). Though Wiley was a member of Congress, his book is exclusively a collection of congressional humorous stories and jokes, and so, for this purpose, it seems appropriate to include it with joke books.

2. These are Alben Barkley (1954), Champ Clark (1920), Samuel Cox ([1880] 1969), Sam Ervin (1983), Brooks Hays (1968), Adam Powell ([1971] 1994), Morris Udall (1988), and James Watson (1936).

3. This book by Senator Wiley of Wisconsin, *Laughing with Congress* (1947), offers a wealth of insights into the public humor of congressional elites at the dawn of the civil rights revolution. However, Wiley added several stories he had collected to those submitted by other members of the Eightieth Congress, and this has consequences for a discussion of congressional racial humor at this time. This is discussed in note 4.

4. Most of the stories involving race for the 1929–1964 period are found in Wiley's *Laughing with Congress* (1947). Though this book is based on stories submitted to him by his contemporaries in the Eightieth Congress, almost 40 percent of the racially themed stories are stories he had heard and collected himself. One such story is about an African American whom he refers to as an "old colored man" and "a real singing Sam." Interestingly, this individual is presented as a rather industrious person (214–15).

A story involving race from Alben Barkley's book *That Reminds Me* (1954) appears in a chapter dealing with the First World War rather than with politics. Nevertheless, it reflects the perception of African Americans by an important leader of this period: "One night in St. Nazaire, for instance, we were walking behind a group of American Negro soldiers who came from Mississippi. They encountered some French native soldiers from Morocco, and tried to strike up a conversation. 'Where you from?' one of the Mississippians asked. He got a reply in very fast and unintelligible French. 'I said, where are you from?' the American repeated with emphasis, and once again came the torrent in French. Finally the Mississippi boy said in disgust: 'You're a hell of a colored man—can't even speak your own language'" (115–16).

5. It is not suggested that any other African American member who has served in Congress would fit into the "trickster" mold. In discussing it here, we are applying it solely to Congressman Powell's behavior. However, we are also analyzing the role of humor in the integration of African Americans into Congress, and, when looked at in this way, his behavior cuts a rather humorous pattern. As a trickster, we must note that his behavior was quite brave at times—indeed, even pathbreaking—but at other times also very questionable, if not downright corrupt.

A white Southern senator, Huey Long, was also known to use the trickster tactic at times. "When a new hospital for the underprivileged was built in Louisiana, Negro politicians complained to Governor Huey Long that there were no Negro nurses there, even though half of the patients were Negro. The governor told them he would fix it, but they wouldn't like the way he did it. He made a big fuss in the media about white nurses being humiliated and lowered by taking care of colored men. Racist talk it was indeed, but a lot of colored nurses got jobs in that hospital, and have had them ever since" (Gingras 1973, 126).

6. A variation of this story is found in Schutz's work (1977a). In this story, Powell is giving a street coroner speech in Harlem in which he "bombastically cited his congressional achievements for blacks, his promises for their progress, and his championship of the downtrodden. A middle-class black, standing in the crowd, became extremely offended at the disparity between Powell's self-panegyric and his notoriously disreputable behavior, particularly because of his warm reception by the poor blacks. Turning to another onlooker, he cried out, 'My God, he's always absent from Congress; he has white and black mistresses on his governmental payroll; he uses our tax money on his expense account for whoring, drinking, and traveling!' His companion replied, 'yeah, man, ain't he cool'" (58n).

7. In his excellent biography of Adam Clayton Powell, Charles V. Hamilton (1991) draws heavily on Myrdal to interpret and evaluate the political life, contributions, and shortcomings of Powell. Among other points, he argues that this American dilemma made it difficult for other contemporary civil rights leaders not to come to the defense of Powell when he was being denied his seat in the House, even though they felt his behavior questionable (485). At the same time, Powell exploited this dilemma for his own purposes.

5

Irreverent Theater:
Congressional Humor and
the Gender Revolution

> It could probably be shown by facts and figures that there is no dis-
> tinctly native American criminal class except Congress.
>
> —Mark Twain

Periods of change provide rich opportunities for humor, and, con-
versely, humor can be drawn on to hasten change. Arthur Koestler
writes that the contrast between current norms and their assumptions and
norms appropriate for the forces of change provide many opportunities
for clashes and new insights. "The confrontation with an alien matrix reveals in a sharp, pitiless light what we failed to see in following our dim
routines; the tacit assumptions hidden in the rules of the game are
dragged into the open. The bisociative shock shatters the frame of com-
placent habits of thinking; the seemingly obvious is made to yield its secret" ([1964] 1989, 73). What are perfectly reasonable expectations under
current norms may be a source of much irony and mirth when juxtaposed
with norms necessitated by changed social forces. Similarly, William Fry
finds much humor in paradoxes, which he defines as "a breakdown in our
logical system." He sees an increase of paradoxes during periods of great
social change, when contrasts between the old and new stand in sharp relief (1987, 42–50).

The waves of change that wash over the country also wash over the institution of Congress, and they create paradoxes between old and new patterns of behavior and expectations within the institution. During times of
great change, new norms and roles need to be negotiated among members
(see Emerson 1969, for a discussion of humor and negotiations). Humor

can play an important role in these negotiations, both in pointing out contrasts between the old and the new and in facilitating the delivery of messages that would be difficult without their humorous content. In one particularly historic instance for Congress, such changes in norms and attitudes were necessitated by the suffragette movement.

WOMEN IN CONGRESS

Over the years, legislatures have been perceived by female members as "men's clubs," "male fraternities," and places for "male bonding" (Kirkpatrick 1974, esp. chap. 6).[1] Congress very much fit into this mold. During the nineteenth century, women were thought of and referred to as the "gentler sex" and frequently were the object of innuendo by members of the all-male Congress. Thus, nineteenth-century congressman Samuel "Sunset" Cox writes:

> Let me, then, refer to some of the occasions and illustrations of this by-play of humor. The gentler sex is a frequent theme. The laughs, however, are too often equivocal and reprehensible. Widows' pensions, the marriage and other relations, are subject to the usual bandy of unexpressed but suggested ribaldry. "My object was to reach the widows on the private calendar," says one. Another asks, "does this bill *embrace* washer-women as well as teamsters?" . . . The stage is not coarser than Congress in this respect, and a gallery of ladies makes no difference. A member says, "It is asserted that a good many of these clerks are married: I have seen the unhappy list." No matter what the subject, whether Topsy or "Thanatopsis," mention "women," and the old joke appears, ineradicably suggestive of something not said. ([1880] 1969, 226–27, emphasis in original)

In Congress prior to the suffragette movement, the formal rules and informal norms presupposed male members. This culture manifested itself in a number of ways. Forms of address were masculine; official prayers by chaplains invoked blessings on male members; security staff and parking attendants were male as were elevator operators; and toilet facilities were built for males. As late as the 1970s, female members of the House complained about the condition and distant location of the single toilet allocated to women members. As well, their access to the House swimming pool was limited to early morning hours, and there were still no female pages as late as the start of the 1970s. Postsuffragette issues included the role of women in Congress, how they would be perceived, how they would be addressed, how they would dress, and what access they would have not only to facilities as basic as toilets but also to congressional exercise rooms and swimming pools.

As more women became members of that august institution, these issues were more and more brought to the fore. In the early years, there was considerable ambivalence, if not resentment, on the part of many male members, owing in part to the fact that many of the early female members were widows who filled the remainder of their respective husbands' terms. Male members often believed that such a woman's method of selection was illegitimate; that the women members in general were lightweights; and that, in any event, the women were focused too narrowly on women's issues. In point of fact, from 1916 until 1940, more than half the female members in Congress were widows who succeeded their husbands, and many of these were from Southern states (Gertzog 1995, 18; see also, tables on 20, 23).

At the same time, in the years immediately following the first appearance of female members, there was considerable concern among suffragettes as to how female members of Congress would be accepted by male members. According to contemporary political journalist Duff Gilfond, Speaker Nickolas Longworth (R-OH, 1902–1931), also known as the "genial czar," set the stage for flowery forms of address: "The courtly Speaker set the precedent. Tenderly referring to the new female members as gentlewomen, he created an atmosphere in which every politician in the House turned into a knight" (1929, 151). Gilfond might have overstated his case a tad. Mixed in with the bouquets, there were plenty ribald and saucy comments, hardly the stuff of gallant knights of yore.

For example, in 1916, Jeanette Rankin (R-MT) became the first woman to be elected to Congress, entering the House just in time to cast an extremely unpopular vote against the United States' entry into World War I. Alben Barkley recalls an anecdote involving her and former Speaker of the House "Uncle" Joe Cannon that illustrates problems faced by early female members of Congress in establishing proper relationships: "During the debate over the declaration of war against Germany in 1917, Uncle Joe, who was back in Congress but by then no longer Speaker, was taking issue with a lady member of the House. He rose and asked, 'Will the lady yield?' She replied graciously, 'The lady will be delighted to yield to the gentleman from Illinois.' Uncle Joe, then in his eighties, thereupon leaned over to the representative sitting next to him, and, in a ferocious stage whisper which could be heard several benches away, said, 'My god! Now that she has yielded, what can I do about it?'" (Barkley 1954, 97–98).

Perhaps political scientist Irwin Gertzog got it right when he wrote, "The image of the congresswoman as a curiosity appears to have influenced the treatment she received from male Representatives. She was patronized, condescended to, and ignored or dismissed by her colleagues, depending upon which of the House rituals was called for by the legislative 'script'" (1995, 56). Paul Boller cites a number of relevant instances.

"There was much applause (and sometimes flowers) when they took the oath of office, and men in the House frequently made remarks about the fair sex in speeches and on occasion ostentatiously deferred to them in debates" (1991, 58). Over time, this pseudochivalrous behavior wore thin with some of the female members. The perfumed forms of address were overdone and were seen by female members as being condescending, even sexist. As Boller goes on to note, "Ohio Republican Francis Bolton, for one, became upset if anyone used the word, Congresswoman, when addressing her. 'I'm a Congressman,' she insisted. 'A poet is not a poetess and an author is not an authoress. It's degrading to call her that.' New Jersey's Mary Norton bristled when a Congressman condescendingly called her 'the lady' during a debate. 'I am not *the lady*,' she said indignantly. 'I am a member of Congress, elected by the Thirteenth New Jersey District'" (59, emphasis in original). Patronizing behavior, however well intended, led to misunderstandings and sometimes playful verbal jousts. "A certain congressman, intending to flatter Mrs. Luce, said of her in the House of Representatives one day: 'She has the best mind of any woman in the House.' Mrs. Luce was enraged by the patronizing tone of the compliment. 'The mind knows no sex,' she retorted. 'If the lady believes that,' remarked a second congressman, 'she doesn't know the mind of the man'" (Fadiman 1985, 370; see also Boller 1991, 163).

Senator Wiley (R-WI), in his book *Laughing with Congress* (1947), includes a chapter reflecting then current attitudes on women: "Women— God Bless Them All (The Fairer Sex at the Joke Fair)." Wiley himself puzzled over the question of the proper form of address for female members of Congress: "the matter of designating lady members of Congress has proven a verbal thorn for many a member of Congress. Shall the ladies be referred to, as at present, 'the gentlewoman from Connecticut or Illinois' or as simply 'the lady' from a particular state, when comment is made to them or about them" (1947, 156)? He quotes extensively from comments made by Representative Gifford (R-MA, 1922–1947) at the start of the Eightieth Congress about the qualities of his new female colleagues:

> As I look over to my left, I see the face of a new lady Member. I wish that all the other lady Members were present. May I say to her, one of the great worries I have in the Congress itself is lest we have too many of you. Although I say this in a somewhat jocular way, still I am a little serious about it.
>
> The lady Members we have today are extremely satisfactory to us. But they, like all women, can talk to us with their eyes and their lips, and when they present to us an apple, it is most difficult to refuse. Even old Adam could not resist. Women have a language all their own. . . . Suppose we had fifty of them. Seemingly, I note flirtations enough now, but what would there be with fifty of them?" (Wiley 1947, 161)

Too many women in Congress?! Fear about the allure of feminine wiles?! Read through the filter of time, Representative Gifford's comments seem archaic and surely grate on contemporary readers.

Some interactions between the sexes made no attempt at chivalry. An anecdote recounted by Wiley has Representative Clifton Woodrum (D-VA) addressing the House "when the veteran Representative, Mrs. Edith Nourse Rogers (R-MA), arose and attempted to interrupt him. 'Will the gentleman yield?' asked Mrs. Rogers. 'Not now,' replied Representative Woodrum. 'It's not very often that we men are in a position where we can make the ladies sit down and keep quiet'" (1947, 157). No doubt Representative Woodrum was attempting to be humorous, but his retort also carried a sting, adding to an undercurrent of tension as members of the two sexes attempted to deal with the gender revolution within Congress.

The matter of dress was also the focus of many negotiations in the process of integrating female members into the congressional fabric. There had long been expectations about the matter of proper dress on the floor, but these applied to men. William "Fishbait" Miller, longtime doorkeeper of the House, cites illustrations of problems of women's dress in a chapter patronizingly entitled, "The Ladies of the Congress—Bless Them All" (1977). A case in point, as he tells it, is that when Miller first met Clare Boothe Luce, she was wearing a short fur coat, regarded by one member as "her fanny freezer." "She was making an entrance by being late and I said, in greeting, 'I'm Fishbait Miller. I want to be your friend and I want you to be my friend' Then I looked around to be sure there were no reporters in the Speaker's Lobby, where we were standing, and I said, 'I am going to show you that I am your friend and tell you something that I hope won't hurt your feelings, but your slip is showing this much.' I made a motion measuring about two inches with my fingers" (69–70). Miller comments that Congresswoman Luce did not speak to him for several months after this but that they became friends eventually, at least by his reckoning.

Some of the discussion by male members reflected latent hostility toward the presence of women in the institution. "The Gentlemen of Congress were not at all pleased when the House was more and more invaded by female members. They especially resented it when one of them acted 'uppity,' as if she had just as much right, if not more, to be there, than they" (Miller 1977, 67). Miller relates an incident involving a West Coast congressman who, on pointing to a congressional woman from the Midwest, comments, "She's a bitchy bitch, ain't she?' . . . I said, 'Well, she's still one of my bosses. I don't know what to say.' 'Well, I'll tell you what I say,' he said irritably and a touch bitterly. 'If her pants were on fire I wouldn't even shoot my water pistol to put the fire out. I'd let her burn up'" (67–68). Sometimes these comments cast female members of Congress in the role of sex objects, never mind how proper they behaved. Again, from Miller,

Another congresswoman who seemed to excite some of our members was Jessie Sumner, a Republican from Illinois whom God had endowed with ample hips and other feminine attributes. There was frequently some talk, especially during the winter, of how nice it would be to be able to go home with a gal like that who could really keep a man warm—"Man, if you lived with that you would never get cold at night." Perhaps Congresswoman Sumner heard of some of the comments on the floor, because she bent over backwards to show how prim and proper she was and opposed to females flaunting their virtues. (71–72)

At times congressional members' feminine beauty was mistaken for a lack of seriousness.

A national public-opinion poll found that after Marlene Dietrich, Congresswoman Luce was deemed to have the most beautiful legs in America, whereupon Walter Winchell reported that when a member teased Clare with this question: "Don't you think it's beneath the dignity of this House to have one of its members voted among the six women in America with the most beautiful legs?" Clare replied, "Don't you realize, Congressman, that you are just falling for some subtle New Deal propaganda designed to distract attention from the end of me that is really functioning." (Shadegg 1970, 177)

Female members of Congress sometimes turned the tables on their male counterparts in negotiations over dress codes. Representative Edith Green (D-OR), who did not suffer fools gladly, tells interviewer Claudia Dreifus about an incident when she found herself on an elevator with an unnamed senator whom she characterized "as one of God's most stupid creatures." "With that great condescension which the male species is so guilty so many times, he literally patted me on the shoulder like a small child, then took hold of my dress and said, 'Myyyyyyyyy! What a p-r-e-t-t-y dress you have!' I couldn't stand it! Oh, that voice, it was unbearable! So I turned to him, and in a voice imitating his, said, 'Myyyyyyyy, what a lovely suit you're wearing. You *are* handsome'" (Dreifus 1972, 17, emphasis in original).

Attitudes change over time, however slowly, and this was reflected in gender humor. Brooks Hays believed he had been sensitized, perhaps even blindsided, to the delicacy of the issue in the early 1930s: "I had my exposure early to the public's unreliable sense of humor, when Secretary of Labor Frances Perkins offered me a job, and I said I turned it down because it was bad enough to have to take orders from a woman at home— to have the same situation at the office would be too much. I did not expect to be taken seriously, but I learned there is a type of mind that can never take a joke at its own expense" (1968, 5). Here, what was intended as innocuous, even self-effacing humor, when it involved a pioneer of the women's movement, was out of bounds. Raucous gender jokes about one's Senate colleagues were clearly beyond the pale by the 1980s, as the rather sardonic Senator Domenici found out. "Peter Domenici (R-AZ) got into trouble for joking, 'I'm blessed with the talent of . . . whipping the electorate to a frenzy. Just like with the singer, Tom Jones, women often throw their panties at me when I speak. It happened again just yesterday. I just don't know what got into Senator (Barbara) Mikulski (D-MD).' This brought down the house but it also brought down the wrath of Mikulski" (Udall 1988, 197).

IRREVERENT THEATER

A couple of exceptionally strong-willed woman members of Congress attempted to change the institution by engaging in what might be called "irreverent theater." A leading characteristic of this theater as it relates to Congress is that its adherents do not accept important parts of the congressional establishment, including prevailing expectations about the proper role of female members, certain policy stances, some of the institutional procedures, forms of personal address, and especially its informal rules. The two practitioners of this theater whom we discuss were skilled at spoken humor and frequently employed it, but they also chose to deliver messages through staging, performances, impression management, and forms of dress (Goffman 1959). They saw themselves as change agents, and they intentionally employed abrasive in-your-face kinds of wit.

Irreverent theater brings important strengths to humor. Those who combine humor and theater provide continuity to their message by developing a clear persona and by dressing up in costumes or uniforms. Consequently, when other members of Congress deal with these agents of change, they have before them—symbolically and dramatically—the full scope of the message that the change agents seek to deliver. In effect, the congresswomen practitioners of irreverent theater combined the power of theater with the power of humor as a way to provoke thought, to ridicule, to deliver messages weighted with irony, and to force certain aspects of Congress and its policies they felt needed to be changed onto the congressional agenda.

The two congresswomen who were especially skilled in the ways of irreverent theater were Representative Bella Abzug (D-NY, 1971–1977) and Representative Patricia Schroeder (D-CO, 1973–1997). Each took pride in her humor, and each also consciously drew on theatrical techniques. In both cases, they leave us with memoirs that allow us to get inside their heads to see how they conceived their objectives and how they managed impressions.

Bella Abzug

Representative Abzug kept a diary during her first year in Congress (1971) entitled *Bella! Ms. Abzug Goes to Washington* (1972), in which she reports her perceptions of what went on and how she felt. One needn't probe deep to identify her persona—she shares it with us in the opening paragraph of her diary, "I've been described as a tough and noisy woman, a prizefighter, a man-hater, you name it. They call me Battling Bella, Mother Courage and a Jewish mother with more complaints than Portnoy. There are those who say I'm impatient, impetuous, uppity, rude, profane, brash and overbearing. Whether I'm any of these things, or all of them, you can decide for yourself. But whatever I am—and this ought to be made very clear at the outset—I am a very serious woman" (3).

Bella was going to be a member of Congress on her own terms. Again, from the introduction to her diary: "I intend, as best I can, to tell it the way I see it. The reason I'm going to be able to do this is *that I have no desire to become a privileged member of 'the Club,'* nor do I care to build a career for myself if it's going to be unrelated to the needs of the people who elected me. What that means, frankly, is that I don't give a damn about being re-elected unless I'm able to do what I want to do. . . . If it proves impossible to do by working within, then I'm prepared to go back outside again—to the streets—and do it from there" (7, emphasis added).

Showing an early flair for drama, Bella staged her own swearing-in ceremony, after the official one, as a way of putting an exclamation point on the message that she would be independent of the institution of Congress. In an entry dated January 21: "After being sworn in on the Floor today, I came out to the Capitol steps, where I conducted my own ceremony. . . . Shirley Chisholm, the black Congresswoman from Brooklyn who is a friend of mine, administered an oath to me in which I pledged 'to work for new priorities to heal the domestic wounds of war and to use our country's wealth for life, not death.' A lot of other Congressmen came out to watch me being sworn in. It's a first, they tell me" (13).

Representative Abzug did not have a great deal of trust in the institution of Congress and its procedures. She was there to change both the way it did business and the business it did. She did not like the seniority system, because she believed it penalized members such as herself, who came from competitive districts in which the constituents expected great change. Nor did she care for her particular committee assignments. Witness this exchange between her and Representative Chet Holifield (D-CA), after he told her that she had been assigned to the conservation subcommittee. She informed him that she didn't like this assignment and that she wanted to be on military affairs, to which he said she did not have enough seniority. Her message to Holifield was blunt: "It seems to me that you would be better off if you understood that seniority is not the only basis upon which committees should function. Had you the guts to put newer members, like myself, on committees which have something to do with our mandates—because most of us are from areas demanding vigorous change—you might have helped the whole rotten Congress, if not the country. You mister, have made a terrible error" (59).

Nor did Bella respect the Democratic caucus in the House and its liberal members. She saw them as being too timid, too ready to strike a compromise with the opposition and the White House. Her disgust with the Democratic caucus and its liberal members boiled over in her March 31 entry. The agenda called for a vote on a motion to require that troops be withdrawn from Vietnam by the end of the year. Instead, an unsatisfactory substitute motion was passed by the caucus. Why? "Number one, because the liberals who voted for the Dent Amendment gave the moderates something they could chew a bit more easily. . . . So they're stupid in addition to not being really committed. Number two—and this really burns me—a few guys who should have been there were absent" (92–94). Indeed, in time she came to believe that she had better relationships with, and more respect for, House conservatives than her liberal colleagues. Above all, she was clear about the issues that were paramount to her: child care for working mothers, an end to the draft, and an end to the war in Vietnam.

What is important to understand about Representative Abzug is that she often staged a performance. The irony about the character of Bella is that it unmistakably communicated the message that she was every chauvinist congressman's worst nightmare. As a female representative she had no intention being demure—not Bella. She was not going to wear a rose in her lapel as Representative (and later Senator) Margaret Chase Smith (R-ME) had done, and she was going to concede nothing to the paternalistic mythology about the "gentle sex" that cluttered the thinking of the male members of Congress. She was not cute, nor was she going to try to be. She was loud and profane, and she was going to break all the furniture necessary to reach her goals. Bella was as tough as any man, and if her colleagues recognized that, along with her considerable skills as a legislator, then she would take it as a compliment. Strangely, though, she seemed to accept her committee chair, Edward Hébert (D-LA), calling her "Bella baby" so long as he respected her legislative abilities.[2] The image she projected is hoary, with irony and ridicule—key elements of humor—and in employing it, she personified the forces of change; she became a harbinger of the transition to the new order that would usher in equality between the sexes in Congress!

An important part of Bella's self-image is that she saw herself as being tough—prepared to do battle with any man and able to curse with the best or the worst of them. As early as February 6, she writes: "In the last several weeks a few items suggesting I use profanity have appeared in the newspapers. I suppose I should deny it, but who would believe me? I'm a very spontaneous and excitable and emotional person, and I do have a way of expressing myself pretty strongly sometimes. Big deal. I don't see where it matters. What matters—all that matters is that I say how I feel, and I always do *that*. The press is stupid to get all excited because I'm prone use a few choice words now and then" (29, emphasis in original). On April 8, she notes that she had to make a few calls to members of the Lindsay administration in New York City, regarding the housing problem. "Finally, I got hold of one of the commissioners—I'd better not mention his name—and my temper ran short and I started to scream and yell at him. A few minutes later my friend Ronnie called back to tell me that this fellow had run down the hall to her claiming I called him a four letter word. Now isn't that ridiculous? A-s-s is only three letters. The man's crying like a baby. Oh, I don't know, I guess it's my cross to bear, these things. I mean, how am I going to do anything if I don't scream and carry on? How else do you get action out of these people" (111–12)? On August 3, Bella complains about having laryngitis, but that hardly slowed her down. She writes in her diary, "Laryngitis or not, this was my day for taking on Wayne Hays from Ohio, a mean, mean, character who's always attacking everybody personally on the Floor. I figured that a bully deserves to be bullied by a bully, and so I couldn't resist my calling" (222). True to expectations, Congressman Hays got into sharp, personal floor exchanges with Representatives James Burke and Ron Dellums. Following the denouement, Bella encountered Hays in the rear of the floor.

> "You know, Wayne," I said, "I think it's pretty crummy of you to go around attacking people personally on the Floor. It's one thing to disagree with somebody, but why attack them so viciously? . . . You may have a right to criticize [Congressman Dellums] . . . but not the way you did. You're always attacking people personally. Like a bully."
> "Well, I may do it to you one day yet," he said.
> "You know what, Wayne?" I said. "You start with me and I'm not sure you're going to get the best of it." (222–23)

She was firmly committed to being as tough and as crude as any male member of Congress, even if it meant crossing swords with the dyspeptic chair of the House Administration Committee.

Bella, always on stage, was acutely aware of her costume. Her character wore floppy hats and loud print dresses and had dark-rimmed glasses that were perched precariously at the end of her nose. Above all, there was the floppy hat! The latter was a point of public speculation when she was elected to the House because of the rules that banned wearing head apparel on the floor. Her costume and that of others received much attention in her diary. On February 6, commenting on the story which ran in the Associated Press (AP), she writes:

> "How about the gossip that [Bella] suggested that the door keeper William 'Fishbait' Miller perform an impossible sexual act [on himself] when he told her she couldn't wear her famous floppy hats—her campaign trademark—on the House Floor?" What the Associated Press doesn't understand, besides the fact that this is absolutely untrue, is that I'm not here to fight about my hats, and if I were, the last guy I would fight with is Fishbait Miller. He's very friendly. He has been since I met him. I was having a very serious discussion about my committee assignment a few weeks ago with Wilber Mills. The door opens up and this little man comes in, a stranger, and kisses me.
> "Whoever you are," I said, "I think this is an over response."
> "I'm Fishbait Miller," he said, "and I wanted to greet you." (29)

Fishbait's version of the story was that Bella, in the presence of others during a reception for new members, had threatened to make the suggestion referred to in the AP story if he asked her to remove her hat before going on the floor (Miller 1977, 79–80). But the important point of the story is the focus on her costume by her and others and how it figured into negotiations regarding how Bella was going to fit into the House of Representatives. In a later entry in her diary, she has this to say on the matter of style: "I want to switch my hair style to something they call the American Afro, the little girl look with curls. As it is, my hair's always a problem. As we all know from the newspapers, I can't wear my hat on the Floor of the House, so I have to take it off and leave it in the vestibule. This usually leaves my hair messy, but to comb it I have to walk what seems like a half mile to the only women's room. A hair style like the American Afro I wouldn't have to comb" (1972, 57–58).

She put her costumes together deliberately, to gain attention from others, and she often critiqued the costumes of others. Early in the session, when making comments in regard to a social function at the White House, she said, "I decided to wear a short dress so I could also wear a hat. I didn't want to deprive the President of that great event. I figured I'd let him see me in my whole regalia. . . . I didn't want to be *too* late. You're supposed to arrive before the President does and I figured it would look too much like a plan to upstage him if I arrived afterwards. Anyhow, I wasn't planning to be smart-alecky" (19–20; emphasis in original). She comments that the pomp at the White House makes the institution seem more British than American, and then she writes about seeing the president: "There He Was. His Wife Too. Even though there wasn't a camera in sight, *he had his makeup on*" (emphasis added). Bella seized the occasion of the reception line to have a critical exchange with the president regarding his Vietnam policy. She comments that the president's arm stiffened when she broached the controversial issue and that he quickly passed her along to Pat Nixon, who said, "'Oh, I've been looking forward to meeting you. . . . I've read all about you and your cute little bonnets'" (20).

It was perhaps inevitable that Bella would draw the ridicule of President Nixon's vice president, Spiro Agnew. She had set herself up as a target for his sarcasm. It happened while Agnew was speaking at a fund-raising dinner in his home state of Maryland. He said, "Republicans should work for adoption of environmental programs, welfare and revenue-sharing and *most importantly, we have to keep Bella Abzug from showing up in Congress in hot pants*" (49; emphasis in original). The next day (March 6) she wrote in her diary, "Everybody's kidding me about Agnew's remark, which I guess is funny in a stupid way. I really can't get angry. Some guys would like to dismiss me with silly comments about my hats or my four-letter words or my figure. Maybe they think that by dwelling on aspects of my flamboyant character . . . they can divert attention from other things I really dwell on such as child care, repeal of the draft and an end to the war. All I say is that anybody who thinks he can take me lightly because I'm fresh and colorful had better watch out" (49).

In an entry dated February 17, Bella's sense of stage presence was evident in her description of a meeting in the White House with President Nixon. She wanted to make points by having a verbal exchange with the president about Vietnam. Notice the elaborate detail she presents as she comments on the choreography of the meeting:

> When the President walked in he went from table to table, shaking every Congressman's hand as they all stood up. I noticed that he kept stealing glances at my table—and at me. He was obviously reluctant to come over, because he knew damn well what was going to happen. It was so evident that he was avoiding us that everyone at the table was kidding me.
>
> For a moment or so, while we were laughing, I lost sight of the President, and then suddenly, out of nowhere, I felt this heavy hand on my shoulder from behind me, pressing down so hard I could hardly turn my head.
>
> Then the voice of America: "All you men and this one charming lady."
>
> The men at the table stood up, and I started to also, but by this time Nixon had both his hands on my shoulders, and he said to me, "Don't get up." Not even a "please." He released one hand to shake hands with the others, but I could still hardly move, let alone turn around and say anything to him.
>
> I must say he bested me. (35–36)

Their meeting had all the movements of a complicated dance, and it is obvious that Nixon was leading!

Writing in 1975, journalist Ken Auletta points out that there was a "good Bella" and "bad Bella." Bad Bella was loud, abrasive, and profane; and sometimes she could be heard berating a colleague at a considerable distance. Good Bella charmed colleagues with her skillful use and appreciation of humor. Ken Auletta writes about the benefits that accrued to Bella because of her "ability to banter, to laugh and make laugh, to apply to what in others might be called 'feminine charm'": "One veteran member of Congress agues that Bella is now more widely accepted in Congress not just because of her brains, but because of her sense of humor. 'Bella and Liz Holtzman (D-NY) are equally bright. But I sit down and tell Bella a story, and she laughs. I tell the same story to Liz and there is no reaction'" (1975, 30).

Bella was so confident of her ability with humor that she staged it to increase receptivity of whatever her message. In the May 11 entry in her diary, she talks about a hard-hitting speech she delivered before the Federal Bar Association in which she took federal lawyers to task for mass arrests, the preventative detention of young war protesters, and "the terrible danger to our civil liberties" that the federal officers' actions posed. "To begin with, I know I have to win them over, so I adjust my tone and presentation to loosen them up. That means, at least when I start out, I have to be completely spontaneous." Bella spars lightly with the person who introduced her and gains a few laughs. Then she goes on to tell the audience a few jokes "until I sensed they were loose enough to be hit hard with what I really wanted to say. All this is not as easy as it sounds. You've got to plug yourself into the audience, sensing its reaction—something in the waves—and go from there. . . . I'm always changing the style, the tone and the nature of my talk to suit the audience so that it will accept what I have to say. . . . Understand something though: Although I'm always proselytizing my audiences, I never change the *substance* of what I have to say to do it, like some guys do. The style may change, but never the message'" (153–55, emphasis in original).

Bella's confidence in her ability to use humor extended to committee meetings. In the October 20 entry we find this: "Everybody says that my one saving grace is that I always have a funny comment to make." (259). Her confidence also shows in her December 15 entry. It deals with the water pollution bill being considered by the Public Works Committee. Governor Nelson Rockefeller testified that the cost of the proposal would be prohibitive. "After I put him through a tough cross-examination, and got him to concede on almost every point, he said, 'The distinguished Representative from New York has questioned my figures. My concern is that in challenging my figures, she has none to substitute except a very beautiful figure of her own.' 'That's one demerit, Governor,' was all I could say to that sexist remark" (284–85).

Later about the same hearing, we find her writing this:

Now, most people would not believe that a freshman would handle a committee that way. All week, I badgered the hell out of them, then, since I had

to leave early, I also asked them for a special request to skip ahead of themselves (they go through the bill page by page) and put in my sex amendment,
which prohibits discrimination on the administration of the program by reason of sex. A lot of people thought it was rather nervy on my part. The rank-
ing Republican member, William Harsha from Ohio, who sits on the tier
above me in this committee, turned around and said, "I want to ask you a
question about this sex amendment."

   I turned to him, peered over my glasses and drawled, "Yes?"

   He burst out laughing and said, "Never mind."

   I got unanimous consent for the sex amendment. (285–86)

By the end of the first session of Congress, as she was summing up her
experience, Bella was satisfied that the persona of "Bella" that she had
created had worked in Congress. "The biggest thing of all that I've done
is to establish myself as a representative of women, of young people, of
minorities, and as an outspoken and uncompromising advocate of turning the nation's priorities around to benefit the poor and lower-income
people. *I symbolize these new priorities because of my actions inside and outside
of Congress*" (301, emphasis added). And she did it her way. She goes on:
"They (my colleagues) understand that I'm not unreasonable. I'm tough
about what I think is right, but I'm not an obstreperous human being. I
fight hard and I try to win. If I don't win, I keep fighting. Anybody who's
ever had anything to do with me—inside Congress or out—knows that if
I feel strongly about something there's no point in stepping on my toes to
change my mind. To the contrary, they stay off my toes as much as they
can because they're afraid I might take them on" (301–2).

Patricia Schroeder

Representative Pat Schroeder's behavior in Congress also comports with
our definition of "irreverent theater." She was dissatisfied with the institution of Congress, which she characterized as a "fraternity house" and its
male members as "bulls." She had little patience for the informal rules of
the House—"they were rules of the bulls for the bulls." She looked for opportunities to focus on what, to her, were the most pressing issues she
could hope to influence, and she employed humor, sexually explicit language, and theatrical techniques to force their consideration. She was not
shy and retiring; she was as loud and outspoken and passionate as necessary to push her issues onto the congressional agenda!

   What she found when she arrived to take her seat in January 1973 was
an institution that she saw as still hopelessly male dominated, down to
the lowest ranks of employment. "When I arrived in Congress, there were
no women working as pages, Capitol police, doorkeepers, or parliamen-
tarians. . . . [Congress] was a cross between a plantation and a fraternity

house—the former being the public persona and the latter its private moments" (1998, 155). About the perception, or misperception, that Congress had of itself prior to the Clarence Thomas hearings in 1991, she writes: "I don't think Congress quite understood how it was perceived as an over-aged frat house until the Clarence Thomas hearings" (158). Leaving little to the reader's imagination as to how she felt about Congress, she entitles chapter 2 of her book "Congressional Bull****."

Pat Schroeder saw the House as a men's club—a guy gulag—that had a distinctive culture that was distinctively unfair to its female members. This was reflected, among other ways, in a system of mentoring. "Anyone watching how the new men in Congress were socialized could see the differences immediately: The senior bulls picked out younger bulls who were like them in ideology and attached themselves as guides and mentors" (30–31). The House, right down to its architecture and interior design, favored male members. "The women in Congress had to wage virtually every battle alone, whether we were fighting for female pages (there were none) or a place where we could pee. . . . There were men's bathrooms right off the main floor of the House, but the ladies' room was at the other end of the earth, constructed out of the original Speaker's lobby in the old Capitol, and it looked as if it hadn't been updated since the inception of plumbing" (31). And there were places in this club that were out of bounds for women members, such as the porch off the House chamber: "The first time I wandered out there for some fresh air during a debate, I could hear a lot of *harrumphing* behind me. It seems that the congressmen liked to pull off their trousers and sunbathe on the chaise longues. They felt 'letting' women on the House floor was enough; we shouldn't also have access to their tanning clinic" (32).

As a new member, Representative Schroeder was concerned about mastering the formal rules, but she seemed even more anxious about learning the informal rules of the "congressional fraternity." "Much of my time was spent trying to master the rules and procedures of the House. It often seemed so stilted and obtuse. But I also spent a lot of time learning about the other sets of rules, the unwritten ones of the *guy gulag*. Those were even harder to ascertain" (36–37, emphasis added). Elsewhere she writes, "I seemed to run over part of the sacred congressional culture on a daily basis. I was oblivious to the rules and the culture" (57–58). Among the informal rules she identifies: guys control the remote to the television in the House cloakroom; many congressmen want Washington as a female-free zone; things are rarely decided on their merits in Washington; regarding extracurricular sexual activities of other members, see no exploits, hear no exploits, and mention no exploits; if one does see or hear such things, one always sides with colleagues, as against their families or members of the staff (37–52).

Schroeder felt the piercing consequences of violating the rule that one does not cross the lines between members and staff when she came to the aid of a staff member who had been fired by Congressman Otto Passman (D-LA). Incident to the staff member's termination, Passman stated in writing that he believed a man could better serve as his administrative assistant, an action Schroeder believed would have been a prima facie violation of sex discrimination laws if the incident had happened in the private sector. Schroeder paid a high price for siding with the staff member: "Crossing the line between congressional member and staff was a huge violation of the institution's unwritten rules. . . . My raising money to help her with legal costs and supporting her case caused many colleagues to shun me forever" (156).

Schroeder was passionate about issues that caused her the most concern—namely, the Vietnam War, what she believed was wasteful defense spending, and the feminist issues of the day, such as equity for woman in health care, family planning, women's right to choice, support for day care, medical leave, sex discrimination in the workplace, and fairness of the federal employees' pension plan to divorced female spouses.

Congresswoman Schroeder's persona was that of a post-1960s working mom who was cleaning house—the House of Representatives, to be specific. "As a young wife and mother, I discovered the frustrations of housework. No matter how much I dusted, vacuumed, changed bed linens and washed dishes, I had to do it again and again. Congressional House work was just the same, with interminable battles and infinite targets" (240–41). Her uniform was consistent with what one would expect of a working mom of her time. She was typically well dressed, frequently in a blazer (but if not, in other attire in good taste), and her salt-and-pepper hair often styled that of a page boy. If one met her in the mall, she would not stand out from the other bustling middle-class suburban housewives. No floppy hats here, but also no rose in her lapel. She was a distinctly modern woman. The irony came in the contrast between the ordinariness of her appearance and the blunt content of her message. She was for the family but for the 1970s model; she was a feminist to the core; and she was against military waste and the Vietnam War. To make her points with her colleagues on the all-male House Armed Services Committee, she was prepared to speak to them at any level. "It's lucky they're not all women or they'd be pregnant all the time, because they never met a weapons system they can say no to" (quoted in Solomon 1998, 62). To be a champion of feminism, she would mince no words in dealing with matters involving sexuality and women's health, the issues of importance to the post-1960s women, even if it meant using sexually explicit language that would cause some of her male colleagues to squirm in their seats. In her, one would find the contrast between appearance of a soccer mom and the audacity of a modern feminist, and those dealing with her would come face-to-face with these two contrasting systems. They could laugh or cry as they chose, but they could not avoid dealing with the issues.

As indicated, Pat Schroeder was pro-family, but she had little respect for the traditional family of conservative mythology. The family that she was championing was the modern two-income family with such concerns as day care, easily prepared meals, hectic schedules, and precocious children. "Its been thrilling to be on the front lines of culture cracking and to shepherd historic changes for women, yet I wonder what the family culture will be like in the twenty-first century. I hope it won't be Martha Stewartville, with those perfectly posed family pictures, neatly framed in her well-ordered home. The chaotic, messy contingencies of family life do not make great photo ops" (Schroeder 1998, 189). She often looked at the helter-skelter pace of her family life with bemusement. "The press would ask what my biggest fear was, and I always answered, 'Losing our housekeeper.' It was a real fear because without one, the Environmental Protection Agency could declare our home a Superfund site" (131). And, "Only our dog got excited when I pulled out the pots and pans. Early on our children thought a balanced meal was holding a hamburger with both hands. I learned not to ask Jim to take me someplace on vacation I hadn't been, for he'd suggest the kitchen" (140). And on the matter of precocious children, she recounted a story of her two-year-old daughter, Jamie, whom she forced to make an appearance at a political function. "The press rushed up to Jamie and asked the first question adults seem to always ask a child. 'What do you want to be when you grow up?' Planting her patent-leathered feet on the floor, batting her eyes and projecting her voice so that nobody in the hall would miss her words, she said, 'I want to be a congresswoman like my mother so I can say "fuck" and "shit" and not get into trouble.' Then she looked at me, smiled and said, 'I told you I didn't want to come'" (140–41). It was with considerable pride, albeit using colorful language, that she tells a story about Jamie as a young adult traveling through China with a college friend. "They often encountered some unpleasant, even hostile behavior. But Jamie found a clever method of protection: She got an eight-millimeter video-camera, and if she encountered any guff, she'd whip it out and say in perfect Chinese, 'Do that again for the police.' A ballsy act" (150).

As the preceding paragraph describing her family illustrates, Representative Schroeder didn't shrink from using four-letter words, in spite of her suburban demeanor, and this was true regarding her work as well. In describing the bluntness of Bella Abzug, she comments, "She never hesitated to roll over people—she didn't give a rat's ass who she offended" (23).[3] Sometimes her language was sexually explicit. When Schroeder and Congressman Ron Dellums (D-CA) were assigned places on the House

Armed Services Committee against the will of its chair, F. Edward Hébert (D-LA), Hébert made them both share a single chair in the committee room since, he said, blacks and women were worth only one-half of a regular member (41). Schroeder recounts the following incident: "Once in a heated debate, Ron said to Hébert, 'There are only two of us who have the balls to stand up against what we all know is wrong.' I tugged on his arm and suggested that 'balls' was not a precisely accurate description of our coalition" (42). Of covering the GOP presidential convention with Pat Buchanan for *Good Morning America* in 1988, she writes that she felt like a wallflower at a hookers' ball. Its nominees, George Bush and Dan Quayle, she characterizes as being members of the "lucky sperm club" (75–76). Schroeder believed her experience at Harvard Law School was good preparation for infiltrating the Capitol Hill boy's club because the five hundred men in her class acted as though the few woman members constituted "estrogen contamination" (93).

Consistent with our conception of irreverent theater, Representative Schroeder had a good sense of staging and performance. When asked to select Colorado's princess to the Cherry Blossom Festival in Washington, D.C., she selected a young woman who had been the baby-sitter for her children, Jo Zirkelbach, assuming she would escort her selection just as other members of Congress would. However, it became a gender matter, as she was told that only men could serve as escorts. She was encouraged to have her husband serve in her place. "Instead, I went to a costume store and bought an Easter bunny suit—there may have been a prohibition against escorts wearing dresses, but there was nothing in the rule book about cottontails. Jo loved the idea and entered the grand state procession of princesses with a giant rabbit on her arm" (60). In another instance of theater, this during the administration of the first President Bush and his "let a thousand points of light burn," she and several members of her congressional staff posed for a goofy picture with Christmas lights draped over their shoulders, to show they had the spirit.

Congresswoman Schroeder was particularly concerned about chemical warfare since large quantities of nerve gas left over from the Korean Conflict were stored at Denver's Stapleton Airport two decades after that conflict ended. Knowing of her concern, Speaker Carl Albert appointed her to attend an international disarmament conference in Geneva. However, Chairman Hébert refused to sign the forms necessary for Schroeder to receive compensation for travel expenses, commenting to inquiries from the press, "She'll get goodies when she behaves like the others" (46). Schroeder's response, "Whacked by one of the bulls, I was supposed to lick my wounds and thereafter serve as a voluntary gofer for the whacker until I was forgiven. But I had no time for repentance or gofering. I went public." She retaliated by making pins with the message "Help, I have

Hébert by the tail" (pronounced A-bear) and by giving them out to col-leagues, explaining the "joys of sitting on half a chair and exposing his other boorish actions" (46–47).

Another instance of expressive theater involves the issue of how female members of Congress would be addressed. Schroeder had tired of Tip O'Neil's treating her differently when he introduced her publicly; so, given the chance to introduce him to a feminist group, she made her point: "'I'm honored to present Millie O'Neil's husband,' I told the crowd. 'We've always marveled at how Tip has been able to combine career and family. Of course, we all know that the most important thing in his life is his four children.' When I looked at Tip, the color was draining from his face. I knew he 'got' my message for the first time" (154). Another instance of what she referred to as "gotcha" politics involves Congressman Robert Sikes (D-FL), chairman of the Defense Appropriations Subcommittee, a Southern conservative who took pride in calling himself a "he-coon." While vacationing in his state over Mother's Day weekend, Schroeder was dragooned off the beach by a military emissary sent by Sikes and made to appear at a fund-raiser in his honor. "Sikes insisted that I speak. So I took the microphone, smiling sweetly. . . . 'I'm sure everyone is sur-prised to see me honoring Bob Sikes because most people know we dis-agree on many issues. But I took time out of my Mother's Day weekend to be here so that Bob's constituents would all know what a fantastic help he has been in trying to get the Equal Rights Amendment passed, and how hard he has worked to keep abortions safe and legal.' The crowd starting murmuring. Sikes looked as if he was going to throw up. . . . The she-coon beat the he-coon that day: No one asked me to stay'" (153).

Representative Schroeder was confident of her ability to create humor. She actively played with ideas and searched the news for good subjects; so, in this respect, she believed Newt Gingrich (R-GA) to be a godsend. "Newt could not seem to learn to engage his brain before starting his mouth. He gave me much more material than I ever had time to work with. I loved it" (212). First, there was Newt's cable television course. In one of his lectures, he proclaims that "'men were better in war because they were like piglets, prone to rolling around in trenches and born with a primal urge to hunt gi-raffes. Life in the trenches would be more difficult for women,' he said, 'be-cause they got infections.' I was fascinated with his theories and got a tran-script. I thought such wisdom should be shared with other members of Congress. I took to the House floor and read the lecture—*great theater* that was picked up on lots of newscasts" (213, emphasis added). Another of Newt's antics too good to pass up occurred when Newt complained bitterly and publicly that he was not given proper seating while traveling with the president on *Air Force One*. Newt was the master of using C-SPAN for par-tisan purposes, so Schroeder believed that this episode was a natural for the free one-minute speeches allowed at the beginning of each day in the House. "I had a fake Oscar in my closet. (My staff used to tease me that I had more props than a Vegas showgirl. . . .) It's a venting session, and it's relayed on C-SPAN, so it gets good play. I got to do one of the one-minute rants for the Democratic side. I pulled out the Oscar to nominate Newt Gingrich for the Best Performance by a Child Actor this year. I didn't feel at all guilty. . . . This little gambit came right out of his legislative terrorism manual!" (214–15).

However, all humorists, skilled or not, face the risk of having messages misinterpreted. Creating humor often involves playfully changing contexts to change meanings. Given an individual's reputation for humor, sometimes audiences themselves, ever alert to identifying humor, will change contexts from that intended by the speaker, and this can result in a humorist's embarrassment. For all her skill, this happened to Congresswoman Schroeder. "One evening, I had four tightly scheduled events, starting with the Gertrude Stein Democratic Club of Washington, a gay and lesbian group. I was giving my regular pep talk about the damage done during the Reagan administration as a clarion call to vote. 'For years,' I said, 'I've felt like the little Dutch boy with his finger in the dike.' Throughout the room, I could hear the whispering and tittering getting louder and louder, and finally my brain processed my huge gaffe. I don't think I could have blushed because there was no blood flowing" (63–64). She comments that she quickly finished her speech and made a rapid exit.

GENDER AND CONGRESS

With the Congress that began in January 1993, about 10 percent of the members were female. As she contemplated the meaning of this change, one of the "old bulls" commented, "Look at what you've done. The place looks like a shopping center" (Schroeder 1998, 121–22). It was clear that the gender revolution had not run its course, but nonetheless the institution had changed appreciably and more change was in the offing.

The gender revolution had confronted Congress with the problem of conflicting expectations about appropriate norms. What had to be addressed were matters such as how perceptions about female members needed to change, how such members would be treated and addressed, and what kind of impact they would have on institutional structures and policies. Humor played a role as Congress grappled with these issues. It provided male members who bridled at the pace of change a way to deliver messages about their feelings without resorting to entrenched opposition to the inevitable. It also afforded female members clever ways to confront issues, short of pitched legislative combat.

Congresswomen Bella Abzug and Pat Schroeder chose to force issues into the open and confront them through the practice of irreverent theater. This tactic was inspired by a profound dissatisfaction with the institution of Congress and its policies. It involved a well-developed sense of drama and staging. The costumes and the raw and sexually explicit language were all part of the tactic. These women were skilled humorists, and they utilized humor extensively; but irreverent theater amplified their message because they came to symbolize the issues they were espousing. The irony and ridicule of their humor was made more pungent through their deliberate use of theatrical techniques.

One might inquire as to how the actions of Congresswomen Abzug and Schroeder and their brand of theater were different from those of the run-of-the-mill congressional mavericks. The primary difference is that Abzug and Schroeder had a clear policy agenda. They would engage in either irreverent theater or skilled legislative practice as commonly understood, whichever served their policy interests. So long as the policy ends were correct, they wanted dearly to be recognized as knowledgeable and responsible practitioners of the arcane art of enacting legislation. Mavericks, in contrast, are much less interested in peer recognition.

NOTES

1. Though Kirkpatrick's book deals primarily with women in state legislatures, her findings resonate with the comments of female members of Congress. When she talks about symbolic put-downs, for instance, she could as well have been talking about experiences of the first female members of Congress. She identifies four such symbolic put-downs: "excluding," such as linguistic conventions that exclude women, for example, "men of the House"; "killing with kindness," including overchivalrous behavior or exaggerated courtesy; "emphasizing differences," that is, excluding women because they are only concerned with a narrow range of women's issues; and "putting women in their place," with comments such as "I can't stand smart women" or "A woman's place is in the home." Probably one of the most flagrant examples of the latter was the "Coya, come home" campaign run against Representative Coya Knutson (D-MN) in 1958 ("Wife in Congress Weighs Call Home," *New York Times*, May 9, 1958, 25; "Representative Knutson Says She'll Run Again," May 10, 1958, 12; and "Minnesota Says: Coya, Come Home," November 6, 1958, 23), ostensibly by her aggrieved husband. She was defeated in her bid for a third term. The title of the November 6 *Times* article was "Minnesota Says: Coya, Come Home." Her husband later admitted that his famous press release had been written by Coya's opponent in the 1958 election (Miller 1977, 74).

2. When Schroeder first met Bella Abzug, the latter said, "I hear you have little kids. You won't be able to do this job" (Schroeder 1998, 22). They eventually became friends, but Bella's comments showed that even she shared the popular male view that being in politics and raising a family did not mix. Of interest, Bella did not run for elective office until her daughters were eighteen and twenty years old and out of the house (Benner 1977, 62).

3. While Bella seemed to think that she got along tolerably well with Congressman Hébert, Representative Schroeder was constantly at odds with him. Bella's assessment of the relationship might not have been reciprocated, however. In one of Schroeder's first conversations with Hébert, he told her, "I hope you aren't going to be a skinny Bella Abzug" (Schroeder 1998, 40).

6

In Their Own Words:
Congressional Humorists
Talk Humor

I feel pretty good about that. The biggest praise a humorist can have, is to get your stuff in the Congressional Record. Just think, my name will be right alongside all those other big humorists.

—Will Rogers

Humor theory holds that context—time, place, culture, and circumstances—is essential to understanding humor. By all accounts, Congresses of the past several decades are characterized by less collegiality than that characteristic of earlier times. The House, while it had its expectations for behavior, had always been a less-disciplined chamber than the Senate. But even the clubby Senate that William White (1956) and Donald Matthews (1960) write about had begun to undergo changes shortly after their works appeared. According to several observers of the Congress, it has become an institution much more individualistic, much less civil, much less manageable. Easy access to television cameras, loosened congressional rules, and the need for individuals to raise significant funds for election to office, had made the Senate, it is said, an institution of equal members (Ehrenhalt 1982; Kassebaum 1988; Roberts 1984). In recent years studies have appeared in the political science literature that proclaim the end of the "senate club" and the "end of comity" in Congress. For example, Barbara Sinclair, in her book *The Transformation of the U.S. Senate* (1989), describes the Senate of the 1950s as an institution characterized by teamwork and clear norms that specified expectations of members. In contrast, she found that by the 1970s the Senate had been transformed into a more individualistic institution, with members more able to pursue their rational self-interest. "The new system that began to emerge during the late 1960s and came into fruition in the 1970s is much more open, less bounded, and less stable; it is characterized by a much larger number and diversity of significant actors, by more fluid and less predictable lines of conflict, and consequently, by a much more intense struggle to gain space on the policy agenda" (5). Eric Uslaner discusses the "comity" in Congress, which he defines as the extension of reciprocity and courtesy within a system of norms, and how it declined in the period between 1970 and 1990. He writes that while the 1950s were a time of civility in Congress, "by the 1980s, the House and the Senate came to resemble day care centers in which colicky babies got their way by screaming to the top of their lungs. An elaborate set of norms emphasizing courtesy and reciprocity that had been in place at least since the 1950s no longer restrained members from making personal attacks on each other" (1993, 5–6). By the mid-1980s and through the 1990s, partisan tensions were ratcheted up several notches. A number of events were symptomatic of the changes—the partisan rejection of the nomination of Robert Bork along with the unusually contentious confirmation of Clarence Thomas to serve on the U.S. Supreme Court; the rejection of John Tower, a former member of the Senate, to be secretary of defense in the first Bush Administration (the first cabinet nomination to be so rejected since 1958); the first change in partisan control of both houses of Congress in over forty years, which took place with the midterm elections of 1994; and the impeachment of President Clinton by the House of Representatives (the first president to be impeached since the Reconstruction period).

It was in these turbulent times that I interviewed nine congresspersons who were members of the 104th and 105th Congresses, which met between 1995 and 1999. Of the nine, four were members of the House of Representatives, and five were from the Senate; and five were Republicans, and four were Democrats.[1] Members interviewed were noted for their use of humor in their work. The interviews were semistructured, conducted over the phone, and taped. I asked the congresspersons such questions as, What do you think are the advantages and disadvantages of humor? What type of humor do you see as the most effective? What topics do you see as off limits for humor? And how do you go about creating humor? (For a list of interview questions, see appendix A.) Most interviews took place in the fall of 1997 and lasted about twenty to twenty-five minutes. The method used to analyze congressional humor is a careful textual analysis of these interviews.

The data for this chapter, then, are the words of the congressional members themselves, as they talked about how they employed humor and how they evaluated that of others. Their thoughts are serious, even analytical, about this type of speech because, to them, it is a serious matter. They used humorous speech carefully and deliberately, but with some trepidation: they knew that humor might benefit them, but they knew as well that it might be taken in a way unintended, to their great detriment. The focus of this study is on how important humor is to Congress, how it is employed in legislative work as it is perceived by members of Congress. What becomes clear as we look at the congresspersons' comments is that, even in these most turbulent of times, these current and recent members, who had reputations as skilled humorists, held on to their belief in the benefits of humor and that they continued to think, even with the intense partisanship in their chamber, that humor was beneficial to the legislative institution.

HUMOR CAN BE GENTLE AND ADVANTAGEOUS

On the topic of the advantages of humor, we find that these skilled practitioners believe that the beneficial consequences of humor are that it "facilitated communication," "placed its user in a more favorable light," "relieved tension," "made people feel good," and that "if a speaker is known for his/her humor, people wait expectantly for your next performance."

The benefit of employing humor is a recurring theme among the congresspersons interviewed. For example, Senator Alan Simpson (R-WY) commented that he sees humor as a way of getting others to listen to one's message: "If you use it right, you can get away with murder. If you misuse it, you can be the subject of ridicule. So the use of humor enables you to open the door or open eyes or open minds, and then, drive your truck right through the gaping hole. So you have opened them up with humor and then you can say something very serious that they will hear because they are receptive to what you are saying" (1997, interview). Senator Robert Dole (R-KS) suggested that "if you use it properly, I think [humor] puts people at ease. If you've got an audience or you walk into some room and it looks quiet and cold and still, you can kind of wake people up. . . . Plus I think it gives people sort of a good feeling about the speaker before they get covered up with speech" (1997, interview).

Several members also mentioned that an advantage of humor is that it breaks up tension. Representative Henry Hyde (R-IL) addressed this benefit: "Oh, I think diffusing a tense situation is one of the most effective uses of humor. Secondly, if one has a reputation for saying clever things, people are going to listen to him because they have a high expectation of something memorable being uttered." Representative Hyde continued with an example of another use of humor: one might be able to avoid an uncomfortable topic. "Humor can diffuse a tense situation, it can fill in the gaps—I remember once I was debating Mickey Leland of Houston, Texas, who was a very able African American member who died tragically in a plane crash in Africa—but I remember I was in a frenzy over some issue or another and he asked me to yield and asked me a question I hadn't the foggiest idea of the answer but he was wearing a red knit tie. And instead of answering his question, I asked the gentleman if that was a necktie or if he had open heart surgery. And everybody laughed and forgot what his question was which was my purpose" (1998, interview).

Senator Pat Roberts (R-KS) cited another benefit of humor: it helps one keep a healthy perspective toward work.

> I think, basically, you take the job seriously but not yourself. And I think if you do that, I think you are in much better shape in terms of your attitude about, you know, what you're trying to accomplish. I know when we went through what I call the "lonesome dove" farm bill trail ride, it took about a year and a half to achieve a dramatic change or a reform of a sixty-year-old farm program. And it got pretty tough, to say the least. Without a sense of humor, without at least approaching some of the problems with some degree of levity, I think we all would have, what, committed hara-kiri on the steps of the Capitol. So it gives you a sense of balance, and I think it serves you well at least in terms of your legislative endeavors. (1998, interview)

These congresspersons found the advantages of humor to the institution of Congress to be similar to those at the individual level; that is, humor breaks up tension and helps to move along congressional business. According to Senator Bumpers (D-AR), "When you're on the floor of the Senate and things get the hottest and most volatile, often if you have the ability to think up a story or use spontaneous humor that you conjure up on the spot, it can have a great alleviating effect on a tense situation" (1997, interview). Senator Roberts agrees that a benefit of humor to Congress is that it can reduce tension. "Oh, there's no question. [Humor] brings you back to reality. It's like in some cases, it really saves the day. And people say, OK, let's take it easy a little bit. Let's don't take ourselves so seriously. And people look at that and I think you need somebody in there who at least will say, now wait a minute folks, let's not get so excited here. It's a pressure valve."

Reflecting on his considerable experience in the House, Representative Hyde commented, "Political humor humanizes Congress. Everybody likes to laugh, if it's a good, healthy laugh, and rather than [as] you say, at somebody's expense. I think people who take themselves so seriously, so grimly, so ponderously, can be awfully boring and ultimately ineffective." Senator Simpson sees humor as the oil that lubricates the legislative machine. "Well, it's kind of the oil that makes the machine run. It's the oil and the grease of government because you can de-fang a situation. There are people who have used it beautifully. All parties, all philosophies, all persuasions. . . . The people who use it and know its worth can ease any situation. And, you know, my mother described humor as the universal solvent against the abrasive elements of life. And it's still a very good point."

SELF-EFFACING HUMOR

Most of the members interviewed felt self-effacing humor was the best kind. Senator Bumpers remarked, "In public speaking, you can ingratiate yourself with self-deprecating humor better than any other way. I cannot remember in my twenty—almost twenty-seven years in politics, ever having made a speech to any group without opening with a couple of good jokes and, as I say, preferably self-deprecating jokes. That does a lot of things: number one, it sort of puts them at ease, it puts them in a good mood, and secondly, you let them know that you don't take yourself too seriously." Representative W. G. "Bill" Hefner (D-NC) answered in much the same vein. "Well, the advantage [of humor] is that it kind of neutralizes any hostility that you might encounter. You know, most people like for their politicians to poke a little fun at themselves and not take themselves too seriously. I've always done that and it can disarm an otherwise hostile audience. I've always used that philosophy; it just comes natural to me" (1997, interview). Senator Conrad Burns (R-MT) offered an example: "I remember making a speech in Cody, Wyoming, one time and I took my eight-year-old daughter with me. And she said, 'Dad, I noticed that you bowed your head before you spoke. What'd you do?' 'Well, I said a little prayer. I asked the Lord to help me, that I would make a good speech, that they would be entertained; I could leave a message, and that I wouldn't offend anybody. And that he would just help me.' And her immediate response was, 'Well, why didn't he?'" (1997, interview).

Senator Simpson rejects the idea that humor must always be at someone else's expense.

> The best humor is the one you tell on yourself. . . . The joke I tell which busts the house down, it doesn't matter how many times they've heard it. . . .You say, by God, things are different out there for us in politics. Went to Cody, Wyoming, my home town. Buffalo Bill founded it. . . . He named the hotel after his daughter, Erma. I'm in the Erma hotel, it's Saturday morning, I got my grubs on, I got my Levis, and my cowboy boots, and I'm about six-ten with those on. And I'm payin' my bill, some guy comes up and says, "Anybody ever tell you, you kinda look like Al Simpson?" I said, "Yeah, they do." He says, "Makes you kind of mad, don't it." They love that.

Senator Bumpers recounted a similar story about sitting next to a woman on an airplane trip.

I was coming back to Washington and there was a lady sitting beside me and she had something that looked like a Gameboy. . . . I was hoping she didn't recognize me because I had a lot of work in my briefcase. She showed no sign of recognition. But after we landed in Washington, she turned to me and said, "Senator Bumpers," and I said "yes." She said, "I have voted for you every time you ever ran; I thought you were just wonderful." And I said, "Well, thank you very much." She said, "And you know something else, when you first ran for governor, I thought you were the best looking man I'd ever seen." And I started sittin' up straight and, you know, tightening my tie and about that time she said, "Man, time takes a toll, doesn't it?" Well, people like that story.

RIDICULE

Though most of our congresspersons emphasized the positive functions of political humor, a few also mentioned that ridicule is one of its important functions, that, if others felt that they might be ridiculed, it gave one a position of power in regard to them. In the first interview with Representative Barney Frank (D-MA), he included *ridicule of opponents* and the *fear of others that you are capable of doing so* as functions of humor (1994, interview). However, by the second interview, he had definitely moved away from ridicule as one of humor's long-term benefits (1998, interview).

Senator Bumpers, as were most others, was wary of humor at other people's expense, but he did go on to tell a story that he classified as borderline ridicule.

Not long ago there was a House member at a gathering where I was in attendance and was on the dais list, and he was too, and he had on a tie but didn't have a coat. And he had on brogans instead of regular black shoes, as politicians are known to wear, and somebody said something about it's really hot today, and he showed that he was smarter than the rest of us by dressing the way he did. And when I got up, I said something about it. I said I got a slightly different take on that. I said, as a matter of fact, when I look at this House member over here, I know now why they call the House of Representatives the lower house. Well, everybody laughed, but I can tell you that's a borderline story because you're having great sport at somebody else's expense. If you're at a toast and roast that's normal; you're expected to be roasting somebody. But if you gratuitously tell a story that is funny but in a way it's also insulting somebody else, you don't help yourself. People will laugh, but they don't think any more of you for telling that story.

One of the things Senator Dole cautioned about was public ridicule of others. "That would be a big mistake to go into an audience and make jokes about any person or whatever." Yet, Senator Dole is noted for his caustic humor. A couple instances come to mind. In the debate on the 1982 tax bill, he commented that Congressman Jack Kemp was trying to get a deduction for hair spray (Frank 1994, interview). When shown a photograph of former presidents Ford, Carter, and Nixon, he quipped, "There they are—See No Evil, Hear No Evil, and Evil" (Udall 1988, 148). During budget discussions, he saw the approach of the Bush negotiating team—Nicholas Brady, secretary of the treasury; Richard Darman, director of Office of Management and Budget; and John Sununu, Bush's chief of staff—and quipped, "Here they come, Nick, Dick, and prick" (Klein and Rosenstiel 1995, 32). In the last case, the authors of the article make the point that Dole is respectful of other senators but cannot accept sneaky or crude behavior or, in the case of Sununu, arrogance.

This raises the question, Why do congresspersons use ridicule if it is an inferior kind of humor? One answer is that ridicule can be defensive. If someone attempts to attack me or my ideas, I might attempt to regain face by ridiculing that person. I might even make an example of that person, thereby giving a warning to others not to attempt to invade my space. Though he clearly prefers self-effacing humor, Representative Hefner spoke to this matter: "You have to have a good sense of humor and you have to have some snappy comebacks; you can't let people take cracks at you all the time. If you can have some humorous comebacks, you know, that neutralizes, like I said, a very hostile audience." Or, ridicule might just happen without forethought, by someone who is adept at humor and cannot resist an opportunity to show off. Again, ridicule might be engaged when an individual is among a small group of good friends; this might explain the example of Dole and the three Bush advisers. Finally, the skillful use of ridicule might be the best way to bring down a formidable adversary who has an overbearing sense of seriousness as Senator Ervin did in the case of Joseph McCarthy during the senate censure hearings of the senator from Wisconsin (Ervin 1983, 162).

Pretentiousness leaves people wide open to ridicule. There is no better instance of this in the annals of Congress than when Representative James Blaine referred to Representative Roscoe Conkling's "turkey-gobbler strut" in floor debate. In doing so, he called attention to Conkling's pomposity and swagger and to Conkling's immense irritation, the imagery followed him for the rest of his public life (see chapter 2 for this and other examples). President U. S. Grant ridiculed Senator Charles Sumner (R-MA) for constantly putting on "learned airs," when he chortled, "The reason Sumner doesn't believe in the Bible is because he didn't write it himself" (Schutz 1977a, 258).[2]

Representative Hyde commented that ridicule can sometimes be disguised. "In debate, on occasion, I like to quote somebody, who said, 'Ignorance is salvageable, but stupid is forever.' If someone has just made a statement and you say that, you're really not calling them stupid, directly, but you are indirectly. There's an art to the perfumed ice pick, which, occasionally happens. I've always used an old Italian saying that you may dress the shepherd in silk, he will still smell of the goat."

THE DANGERS OF HUMOR

Several of the legislators interviewed mentioned that humor can be dangerous. If one tries to be humorous too often, one will not be taken seriously. Representative Frank commented that if you try to be funny too often, "you will just overdo it and look unserious to people. There's a fine line. People do expect some substance from politicians, and if you seem too much in the humor vein, you can have your seriousness diminished" (1998, interview). Worse yet, constituents might think you are "goofy." Senator Simpson also commented on this: "Some people can, you know, look at your humor and say, 'You know . . . that's just off the wall,' or 'That guy is crazy as hell,' that is the hazard."

If one is not good at humor, attempts to use it are likely to fall flat. Some people appreciate humor but are not good at it. Senator Dole pointed out, "They may not use it, but they understand it. I think it's more timing than anything . . . how quickly you react and how you tell it. I think you can get three people telling the same story and it might be funny for one, maybe a little funny for the second, and maybe not at all funny for the third guy. So there are differences in the way it's told and the way you sort of get an audience into it."

But, then, any attempt at humor is a calculated risk, even for skilled humorists. What is intended to be humorous or ironic might not be understood in that light by the intended audience. In response to a question about humor that backfired, Senator Roberts commented: "I've been pretty fortunate in terms of trying to gauge an audience beforehand. I think what happens some of the time is that you'll say something, it will be a little too quick or it will be too obtuse and people will just look at you like what on earth has he said and why does that make any sense? And I think that has happened to me several times—at hearings."

With even the best of credentials and the purest of motives, humor can be misunderstood. For instance, Senator Dole, who was seriously wounded during the Second World War, used to tell the story about why he went into politics. "I used to tell a story about a fellow who had a head injury in the war. And I always related myself, you know . . . it's been so long, I've stopped using it . . . [that I] had a head injury and went into politics, or something or other. But somebody wrote me a letter and said, you know, you have offended me. I like you, but you've offended me because I had a son or somebody with a head injury. You never really know. People may laugh and the audience may think it's funny, but you may be offending somebody. You have to be very careful about anybody's physical disability . . . so that's sort of off limits." Here is a case where Senator Dole was offering self-effacing humor, and, unbeknown to him, somebody took umbrage.

WHAT IS POLITICALLY CORRECT?

By the mid-1990s members of Congress had been sensitized to matters of political correctness. When asked what topics are out of bounds for political humor, members I interviewed were ready with a list of proscribed topics. Notions of what is considered to be "politically correct" weighed heavily on them. Senator Simpson took exception to humor of a personal nature and humor that is tasteless. "So if you want to get up and make fun of people, like talk shows do now, making fun of others, that's not humor. I think that is cruel, and I don't like it. And of course, there is totally tasteless humor. I've done some humor about cows and bulls and horses and so on. But raw, tasteless humor is to be guarded against." Senator Bumpers identified jokes at the expense of others, jokes of a sexual nature, and ethnic jokes as being out of bounds. "Anything even bordering on vulgarity or profanity is pretty much off limits," and regarding ethic jokes, "Those are absolutely taboo. I don't care if you're talking to an audience that is all Italian, you don't tell a Jewish joke or vice versa. That kind of humor is just out of bounds." But he added, "You might use it in the cloakroom." When considered collectively, their lists of taboo topics include humor about races, genders, homosexuals, ethnic groups, and religion; humor that makes fun of somebody else; off-color jokes; jokes about family; about the physical appearance of others; and profanity.

Most of the members I interviewed mentioned three or four of these items, though the scope of what they included varied, as did the way they felt about political correctness (PC). For example, Senator Roberts has a rather encompassing view of PC, and he quite clearly believes that things have gone too far toward sensitivity and limiting speech. "Boy, I don't know. I think the pasture is so wide now that, I mean, there's almost no fences. I mean, you have to stop and think about almost anything that you're going to say—and more especially today with all the hoo-rah. . . . You just have to be very mindful of it. I think we have gone a little nuts in that particular area. But, you know, times change." He cited an example of PC gone awry.

One of the first things that I was fond of saying was that I'm from Dodge City, Kansas. And we're a little different out in Dodge, we're pretty candid about, you know, how we approach things and you know, down to Earth. And I would pause, and I would say, oh, for instance, "We shot a vegetarian the other day" and I said, "It wasn't anything personal. He had broccoli right on him; he was in the city limits." And I said, "He wasn't hurt too bad." And at any rate, everybody enjoyed that, except the first time that I addressed the senior executive service at the Department of Agriculture, who came up to hear about their comportment in regards to hearings. And they were asking what would be appropriate, what would not be appropriate, what about their preparation—we did not get into that—but I went through my typical—some would say—what, *Hee Haw,* I guess, introduction—that really dates me. But at any rate, I said that, and at the end of the session, a lady in the back got up and informed me that she was a vegetarian. And that diet certainly would result in lower cholesterol and et cetera, et cetera; it was very healthy and what advice did I have for her. And I said, "Ma'am, if I were you, I'd get the hell out of Dodge." Well, that prompted a response like, "You, you have just had it." I was told by my staff afterwards, "Now look. You are now chair of the Ag Committee. You've got to behave yourself." So I think there's a downside risk . . . when people certainly believe the issues of the day deserve serious attention and serious consideration—and they do—so you always run the risk of offending somebody if they think you're taking it too lightly. And you have to be careful today about what is PC and what isn't PC.

Representative Hyde found he had gone too far when he repeated a line he had remembered from a fellow member of the House, Representative Billy Tauzin (R-LA). He was doing a *Firing Line* program with Bill Buckley at the University of South Carolina.

On the other panel was Harriet Woods, who is chair of the Woman's Political Caucus. And I was needling her because they pretend they are for all women, but they are only for liberal women. Phyllis Schafley would be anathema to them. So I was asking her during the television show if she ever endorsed any conservative—well, what is a women's political caucus for?—to elect more women to Congress. And I said, "Well, have you ever elected, endorsed, a conservative woman?" And then I remembered Tauzin's line, which I wish I never had. I said, "Why, to me," I said, "there are those who say, if you go to the Floor of the House of Representatives, there are so many women there now, it looks like a mall." And, oh . . . the roof came down. The audience did everything but hiss. I think it's a funny line, but it isn't acceptable in polite society. It fell on its face.

Sometimes it takes a herculean effort to avoid being politically incorrect. Senator Burns told a story about a friend who was trying to adjust to the new rules of political correctness. "I have a friend and he was going to make a speech and he says, 'I gotta quit telling these [ethnic stories], Conrad.' And I said, 'Well, if you have to tell one, tell it on the Babylonians.' I said, 'They haven't been around for about four thousand years.' And he says, 'I think I'll try that.' So he went to Bismarck, North Dakota, of all places. When he came back, I said, 'Charlie, how'd it go?' And he said, 'Well, that didn't work.' And I said, 'What do you mean?' He said, 'Well I told this story about these two Babylonians, walking down the street, Lars and Sven.'"

Representative Barney Frank probably has the clearest conception of what kind of political humor is off-limits. "Topics that are off-limits for politics in general. If it's off-limits for serious conversation, it's off-limits for humor. Political humor doesn't give you a license to say things that you couldn't otherwise say" (1994, interview).

Representative Pat Schroeder (D-CO) has her ideas about what is out of bounds. Although she believes the list of off-limit topics to be broad, she clearly thinks that people ought to be sensitive in employing humor. "Well, you have to be incredibly careful. . . . Ethnic jokes and those types of things are just totally off limits. . . . [The locker-room-type] of joke doesn't work real well either" (1997, interview). Though women's groups are quite sensitive about males' humorous references to females, females do not place similar limits on their humor about themselves. Using blunt gender humor is a way of putting feminine issues such as breast cancer and women's choice on the public agenda, and for some female members of Congress, it is a way of highlighting the masculine nature of the legislative culture. Thus, Representative Schroeder did make references to specifically female concerns, including the female anatomy, which most male members would probably not hazard. In a public lecture, she offered a couple of examples: "If women were smarter than men, they wouldn't wear clothes that button in the back" and "When I was asked for the eightieth time how I could both be in Congress and raise small children, I said, 'I have a brain and a uterus, and they both work'" (1997, public lecture, Columbia, Mo.).

OCCASIONS FOR HUMOR

When asked about situations in which humor is most and least likely, there seems to be a continuum reflecting the publicness of the arena and the gravity of the issue. Thus, members agree that humor is most likely to take place in congressional offices and committee hearings, and least likely during consideration of major issues on the floor.

Senator Simpson thinks that humor is more likely to happen in Senate offices: "Well, to me it is [likely] because you've got young people there, and they are probably talking about the boss or . . . some pompous guy somewhere, and there are plenty of them around. So I imagine that's what I would be doing if I were a young staffer" (1997, interview). Representative Hyde also commented about the likelihood of humor in congressional offices: "Yeah, we kid around. There's a lot to kid about. Constituents come in with some pretty strange requests. I have geese wandering over my district—the golf courses. I had a woman call up and say, 'Those are Canadian Geese aren't they?' I said, 'Yeah.' She said, 'Well, what's the Congressman doing about getting Canada to take their geese back.' I mean that kept us going for a week."

The congresspersons we interviewed also thought humor was likely to come about during committee deliberations. Members of committees know other members, and they all have ample opportunities to engage in humor. What is significant about this observation is that many important decisions are made at the committee level. According to Senator Dole, "You have a chance to give and take then. It's sort of like some of those talk shows. One Democrat or one Republican or two of them sort of bantering back and forth on an amendment or something. Or introducing witnesses. There are a lot of laughs everyday in Congress. I mean just the fact that we meet makes people laugh." Asked about committee hearings, Senator Bumpers asserted, "Oh yes, that's when we get the most humor around here."

During quorum calls is another likely time for joking and swapping stories. According to Senator Dole, "Well, during quorum calls, of course, nobody is speaking on the floor, but you're back in the cloakroom, poppin' off to each other. That's a good time; that's the time you have Simpson and Bumpers and stories." On the House side, Representative Hyde agrees that the quorum call is a time for "meaningless babble" and exchanging stories.

Whether humor occurs during floor debate on major issues depends on the nature of the issue. If the topic is serious and controversial, such as abortion or prayer in the schools, there is not likely to be much humor. Regarding debates on such weighty, emotional issues, Senator Dole commented, "There wouldn't be any humor at all. There shouldn't be." However, on some serious topics, such as defense and the budget, which are not as charged with emotion, there may be quite a bit of humor. Representative Hefner commented, "It all depends on the issue. If you're . . . debating abortion or something of that nature, it wouldn't be very likely. If you're talking about the defense budget or something like that—I remember somebody made the point on the B-2, we're going to spend twenty billion dollars on a plane you couldn't fly in the rain. And the comment was made, 'Well, you don't expect us to take the twenty-billion-dollar plane out in the rain in the first place do you? We're not going to take it out in bad weather.'" In response to whether humor is likely during floor consideration of major issues, Representative Hyde says, "Not very likely, depending on what somebody says or if somebody does something weird. There's an intensity level that is there if you're debating something that is very volatile or controversial."

THINKING ABOUT HUMOR

When asked how they thought of humor, several of the members of Congress whom I interviewed drew on one of two analogies: that humor was like creating drama or that it was like painting a picture. Congressman Frank, alluding to his friendship with the late congressman and former actor Sonny Bono (R-CA), made the case for the relevance of the stage to political humor. "I got to know Sonny Bono, who was here just a year. And I was struck by his insights into how members of Congress appeal to each other, based on his understanding of how performers appeal to audiences. . . . In both cases, you are trying to ingratiate yourself. I mean, you almost always want people to like you. Sometimes you want them to fear you—but Machiavelli to the contrary—over the long term, it is better to be loved than feared. And stress that. So humor makes other people like you" (1998, interview). Some emphasize such intangibles as appearance, timing, and "in-character performance" as being important to political humor. Representative Hyde, in expressing his admiration for Senator Simpson, said, "He was a caricature anyway. I mean he was tall and angular and that high forehead he had and those eyes. But he had a gift for telling stories because he loved them, and he could tell them well. He dramatized them well." Senator Simpson himself stressed that timing and staging as well as feeling the story are important to a story's success. "I've had guys come up to me and say, 'Hey, you tell us some good stories, so give me a couple. I'm going to use them tonight at some banquet.' And then he will come back, and he'll say, 'God, I used that joke, and it never went anywhere.' Well, it probably didn't because it's not your joke. Tell a joke that *you* love, and when you're telling it, you're smiling. When you're telling it, you're at ease. When you're telling it, you're eyes are crinkled because *you know* it's going to be funny because *you* love it. Important point."

Politicians cannot separate themselves from the consequences of the message that their humor carries. Representative Frank clearly sees the difference between the freedom of actors and writers, on the one hand, and politicians, on the other: "A comedian on stage or a playwright or a scriptwriter can put words in people's mouths or mouth words himself or herself and not have to stand behind them. When you are a politician, and you make or repeat a joke, you're being charged with some of those sentiments, most of the time" (1998, interview). Senator Bumpers also sees this difference between the theater and politics: "People in the acting profession, for example, can get by with things that politicians cannot get away with. They have to keep their humor very clean."

Representative Schroeder said that, in developing humor, she attempts to paint a picture or create a cartoon. When responding to the question of what actions or ingredients she looked for in creating humor, she said,

"Well, I tend to work more in word pictures. You know, I am the one who came up with the 'Teflon presidency' and things like that. I mean, I am always looking for 'How do I find a few words that would be like a political cartoon?' that would grab the concept you are trying to cut through."

Of interest, Congresswoman Schroeder was the only female included among the members of Congress whom I interviewed. She commented on the difficulties that political humor poses for women while pointing to a difference between female humorists in politics and entertainment: "I think that is why you don't see as many woman comedians and such. Humor is awfully hard for women to do very well. . . . If you look at women's humor, whether it's Joan Rivers or someone else, basically all she does is sit around and trash other people, you know . . . and as a politician, you could *not* do that."

STORYTELLERS VERSUS QUIPSTERS

Those congresspersons included among our legislative humorists tend to fall into two styles of humor: the storytellers and the quipsters. Storytelling has an honored tradition in American politics. Abraham Lincoln is probably its best-known practitioner, but many politicians throughout the years have prided themselves on their ability to use stories to make a point. When they use this approach to humor, they are not spared of the need to be spontaneous. Indeed, few things are more disastrous than a story told out of context. When a situation comes up to which they want to speak, they need to sort through their store of tales to find just the right one; then they need to adapt it to fit the context, to bring a perspective that they believe to be to their advantage. In the process, they may show another facet of the problem; they may reframe the issue completely; they may also make a protagonist intending to be serious look a little silly; or, again, they may bring self-effacing humor to bear. The stories may originate from a collection of joke books, experience, or a personal notebook of humor. Sometimes they are attributed to different people, and sometimes the facts of the story are changed to meet the needs of the teller or the situation. The critical part—the punch line—remains the same, however.

On the topic of how stories get changed with retelling, Senator Roberts commented on how the same story is frequently attributed to different sources. "You know we all plagiarize to beat the band, you know, with humor, and all you do is change the joke around. As a matter of fact, I was walking with Thad Cochran [R-MS] over in London, and we were part of the interparliamentary group, and we took a little time off to go over to— I don't remember now where we were—it was some museum that we wanted to see, and he got to telling some stories out of Mississippi, and I would say, 'Well that's like the one in Kansas where so and so . . . now Frank Carlson started that story,' and he'd say, 'Well, he didn't start that, that was Herman Talmadge [D-GA].' It's the same stuff."

Of the members of Congress whom I interviewed, those who were especially known for their storytelling acumen include Senators Simpson, Burns, and Bumpers; and Representative Hefner. On the matter of the need for spontaneity, Representative Hefner commented, "In the twenty-two, twenty-four years I've been there, I don't think I've delivered a half-dozen written speeches. I just operate from little notes and things. My wife says I write all my speeches on the back of envelopes." Representative Hefner prides himself in representing the common folks in the Eighth Congressional District of North Carolina. Hence, his store of humor tends toward folksiness, which helps him frame the issue and make the points he intends to make.

> Most of the jokes and things that I do . . . I sort of stockpiled in my mind over the years from when I was growing up and things that were funny to me and stories that you can tell, you can embellish them a little bit if people find them funny, like . . . "It's just like growing up when you were a kid and talk about how bad things were, you know. And then, like sleeping six in the bed; we had to sleep across the bed. And the bad part was we had a bed wetter. And sometimes we'd wake up in the summer time, and there'd be a rainbow in the room." That's pretty down-home corny humor, but there are many places you can use it.

In criticizing a $189 billion Republican tax-cut plan in 1995, he commented, "This package is like the lady that had an ugly baby that was so ugly, she had to tie a pork chop around its neck to get the dog to play with it. That is how ugly this bill is" (Duncan and Lawrence 1997, 1080).

Representative Hefner was aware that he had to tailor his humor to his audience. "I think you have to realize that any jokes you're going tell or situations you're going to get into, you have to be pretty sure they are ones people that are there can relate to. Like if you talk about how you were raised many years ago, you better make sure that there's some folks that are reasonably close to that age group, because if you've got people that are much, much younger, they don't know how to relate to, in the days when you didn't have electric lights and all this sort of thing."

Senator Bumpers agrees that fitting the humor to the audience is crucial. "Well, you have to measure your audience. If you're talking to a farm group, you use one kind of humor. If you're talking to a chamber of commerce banquet, you use something else. If you're talking to a bunch of school teachers, you use something else. I've always tried to use humor that was relative to the group I was talking to. Not only relative but highly relevant to the kinds of work they deal with every day." He also discussed the geographical basis of humor. "Humor tends to have a geographical base too. For example, in my state, some of the stories you can tell, some of the stories I have told, are very funny in Eastern Arkansas and not funny at all in Western Arkansas."

Humor that members of Congress use is likely to reflect the region they represent. For example, Senator Burns talked about being asked by constituents what his impressions of Washington, D.C., were.

> And I always tell them about the ol' cowboy up here after we gathered some cattle one time and we were restin' our horses and he said, "You see up there in the ol' Yellowstone River. There's an old log comin' down the river you know." "And," he said, "see that old log on the river?" And I said, "yeah." He says, "Conrad, on that log there are ten thousand ants. And every one of them thinks they're steering it." I said, "That's Washington, D.C. I never ran into so many super egos in my life as there are there. Phones ringing, doors banging; so many important people and yet they're on that same log and everybody thinks they're steering it."

The fact that humor has to be adapted to a specific audience makes purchasing jokes rather risky. Senator Simpson spoke to the dangers.

> Yeah, I've seen guys who hired a speech humorist from California or the West Coast to do an event in Washington, D.C., and that won't get you there. I mean, humor in New York is different than humor in Washington. Humor in LA is totally different than humor in Washington. And where they lay an egg is where they get started with it and then just don't stop. . . . It's when you get into one, and you just plow ahead and there's no response, and then you start getting defensive with the audience. And you say, "Maybe if you went home and rested a while, you would understand that one, or maybe tomorrow morning, you know, you'll pick it up." Well, then, by that time, they're saying, "Look asshole, shut up and sit down."

Quipsters must respond to the immediate situation without the store of humorous tales. Thus, when they wish to use humor to help them make a point in a situation immediately before them, they have to analyze the elements of the context, come up with just the right line for the point they intend to make, and hopefully not offend anyone or seem mean-spirited. It is a tough assignment. The material of the storytellers may be prescreened, to be certain if it is politically correct. The quipsters must make that judgment at the same instant they are creating the humorous response.

Representative Hyde found his humor in the situations as they arose. "Humor is more spontaneity than anything else. During a committee session, people seek recognition; they make remarks and situations arise that lend themselves to some humorous analysis. . . . You don't look for them and they never happen the way you want them."

Representative Frank, who is often credited with having one of the quickest minds in Congress, looked for surprise in creating humor out of evolving situations: "One of the key elements, of course, for successful humor is that it is not expected. If it's too obvious and predictable, it's not going to be funny. I mean, if it's a pleasurable sound, the fact that it's obvious or predictable is not a problem. But if you are trying to be funny, then it is. You know, you can evoke emotion. I guess surprise is more important to humor than to almost any other thing you might be trying to do" (1998, interview). For him, the best humor is spontaneous, not prepared. If you come with prepared jokes, you are likely to force them into your message, and they do not go over well with the audience. The best humor arises from the situation; it is up to the would-be humorist to recognize the moment and make the best of it (1994, interview).

A problem about the humor of quipsters is that it often does not survive long. This point is made by Representative Frank: "I also think that good humor doesn't carry over well, even by two hours. The kind of humor that I find most amenable just doesn't survive the moment; it's kind of a fragile thing" (1998, interview).

Humor involves a kind of play. Some of the legislators whom I interviewed report carrying on an internal conversation of humorous possibilities. For example, they might ask themselves, "What if I try to juxtapose these two items; or what if I switch these homonyms to create humorous changes of meaning in the context; or what if I creatively change the train of thought to change the emphasis from X to Y with humorous intent?"

Representative Hefner reported on this "internal conversation of gestures" (Mead [1934] 1962). "I travel a lot by myself. And I don't know if it's weird or not. But I get to thinking about a situation and I will say to myself, this would be hilarious. I want to try remember this; I want to try to use this somewhere because it would be hilarious. And then a lot of times I'll forget it, but sometimes it will come up and somebody will make a statement in a speech or what have you, and I'll say, I know how I can use that, and I'll write a little comeback on that or what have you" (Hefner 1997, interview).

The play continues until the humorist receives feedback. According to Congressman Frank, "You get up to speak and you have to gauge the audience, and you can sometimes get a sense early on that this is not an audience in the mood to laugh. Sometimes what I find is that people just don't think they are supposed to laugh, that they may think this is an occasion of high seriousness and they just—it's out of sync. So there are times when I will try a couple of jokes, and if that doesn't work, you try to pick up on that and back away from it" (1998, interview).

Even quipsters are likely to carry some choice lines with them to be used at the ready, especially when they are asked to give public speeches, which is often. Senator Dole addressed this situation:

I think I like to be prepared. You've got to have a few. . . . I think Bob Hope told me once, he was still using good stuff he'd been using for twenty-five years, so you don't want to worry about telling your joke twice 'cause you've got a different audience. It's like dipping into the ocean with a teaspoon; you're never going to cover everybody. And so, I think that's another [ingredient of humor]. Don't be afraid to tell it again. And keep it short, keep it simple so people aren't leaning over to hear it. A lot of it's timing and how you do it and how people think of you.

When asked if he had any sure formulas for humor, Representative Hyde responded,

Not really. I think there are a few things. . . . any congressman has to do a lot of public speaking. And I think everyone should have a definition of a politician— my favorite one—a politician is someone who can accuse his opponent of duplicity without appearing envious. . . . And oh, dear, there was this great story about William Allen White—the editor of the *Emporia Gazette*. Many years ago he was attending a Democratic dinner, and he was asked to give the invocation, and he begged off and the master of ceremonies asked him why, and he said, "Frankly, I don't want God to know I'm here."

But even when using these "ready lines," the deliverers have to observe the usual rules of humor; that is, they have to have a concern for the timing, timeliness, audience, situation, and so on.

THE HUMORISTS

It is likely that many, if not most, members of Congress possess a sense of humor. They appreciate the quickness of mind as their colleagues engage in lively repartee in committees and on the floor. It is also likely that they are able to take the third-party perspective—that is, to get outside themselves and see the humor of their situation, as a dispassionate analyst might see it. They express themselves through skillful use of the language. Their situation often seems uncertain, if not hopeless, and their work is frequently subjected to severe criticism. To survive, many take refuge in contemplating the ridiculousness of their being; in effect, they laugh to keep from crying.

At any given time, however, it is likely that the truly skilled users of humor in Congress will number no more than a half-dozen members, give or take a few. Of these, only a select few will be remembered after a couple of decades for their humor. The users of humor form an elite group, of sorts. They know one another. They critique one another's performances, and they learn from one another what will work and what is out of bounds. They are likely to agree that the ability to use humor is a gift.

Party lines do not divide when it comes to appreciating the craft of finely honed humor. Republicans admire Democrats who are skilled in using it, and vice versa.

Members whom I interviewed know one another, and they as well evaluate one another's performances. For instance, Senator Bumpers said of Senator Simpson, "Alan Simpson has the facial expressions and the mannerisms of telling stories that things that are not all that funny become funny simply because of the way he tells them and the mannerisms he uses in telling them." Senator Bumpers shares the view with several others that Senator Dole is one of the best users of spontaneous humor but that he has a tendency to become a bit acerbic. "When it comes to spontaneity, Bob Dole is about the best I've heard. Sometimes his humor is rather caustic, but his mind is razor sharp where humor is concerned." Senator Dole, too, evaluates the style of Bumpers and other storytellers. "Well, Dale's a great storyteller. You have to sort of categorize them. . . . He and Simpson are really a pair to draw from. And they just love to tell stories. They could tell stories for hours. I couldn't tell five stories, but I've heard Simpson tell five hundred." Of Hyde, Senator Roberts said, "He's got a classical sense of humor. Very, very witty fellow, but it's a real classical sense of humor."

These members of Congress evaluate themselves in relation to others. We just saw Senator Dole compare himself to the storytellers. Here, Representative Hyde employs a scale of ten to compare himself with Congressman Frank: "Some people just think funny. They see humor in things and there is humor, but most people wouldn't see it. . . . On a scale of ten, I maybe have a four or a five. Barney is about a seven on a scale of ten in terms of being able to squeeze some humor or some irony out of a given remark."

The storytellers admire the quipsters, and vice versa. Senator Bumpers said, "Most of the best humor is original and spontaneous. I've never sat around consciously trying to think of a funny retort or something funny to say. But I can tell you that while that kind of humor is wonderful, there are very few people who have the ability to spontaneously say something really funny. Therefore, most of us use stories that are appropriate for the moment, that we can just pull out of the long vocabulary of stories." The quipsters also admire the storytellers, but the former are quick to assert that they can neither remember stories nor tell stories. Senator Dole commented, "I'm not a storyteller. Some people get up and tell long stories. I'm more of a one-liner or quipper, or whatever you call it."

There was a great deal of agreement that Representative Traficant used humor that was a bit too raw. Senator Simpson commented about him, "He gets a little rambunctious. He can kind of get off the wall humor like [Congressman Robert] Dornan. So you want to watch that kind of humor;

that will get you in trouble." In responding to a question about the humor of various members of Congress, Senator Dole opines, "I think Barney's funny from time to time. Traficant is . . . well, different." Senator Pat Roberts was also leery of Traficant's humor. "Oh, he's a wild man. He's just, you don't know what's going to come out."[3]

A number of members of Congress commented that the ability to use humor in their work was a gift. Although it is not clear that they literally thought it was a God-given gift, it is clear that they thought it was a valuable talent and that only the few had it. Thus, Representative Hyde, in talking about the dangers of using humor, allowed, "Unless you're very good at it—and political humor is an art, an almost gift rather than an acquired faculty—it can trivialize you, characterize you as an insincere or an unserious . . . person." Senator Bumpers speaks of humor as a God-given gift: "You can talk about this, but it is a natural gift; it's a God-given talent and some people have it and some people don't." Representative Hefner commented on the small number of politicians who can use humor successfully: "There's a few [politicians] who can be very entertaining with humor. I think it serves people well. Bill Clinton can't; he will occasionally get off a good line but not very often. Jimmy Carter had no humor whatsoever. Tip O'Neill had some great stories."

Members who were noted users of humor admire other users, regardless of party lines. For instance, Senator Pat Roberts, who is Republican, commented about when he served in the House with Barney Frank, who is a Democrat: "It's just like Barney. I knew darn well if I was going to maybe interrupt him during a committee hearing or on the floor. . . . You had better be prepared. And I don't know how you prepare for something like that. You just have to have your wits about you and of course, he's like Zorro." And the Republican chair of the House Judiciary Committee, Henry Hyde, said of fellow committee member Democrat Barney Frank, "This again is an attribute that Barney Frank possesses in abundance: the ability to quickly respond. He talks so fast; once in debate in the last few weeks, I said that it's unfair debating Mr. Frank because in three minutes he gets twenty minutes worth of argument. And his response was 'it isn't that I talk too fast, you listen too slow.'" In response about his respect for Representative Frank, "I respect his brains. He's got them; he's really good."

Senator Burns, who is Republican, expressed a similar respect for Senator Bumpers, a Democrat: "Dale and I haven't voted together probably more than, I bet, you six times all the time I have served with him. But I have a high regard for Dale because he does have such a great sense of humor. He is a man of great dedication to . . . his personal philosophy, and I respect people like that."

THE MEDIA MAKES USING HUMOR DIFFICULT

Sometimes humor is picked up by the media and its context is lost, leading to misunderstandings. Senator Bumpers raised this issue: "Well, I can tell you, the dangers are numerous, but the thing that has caused me grief from time-to-time is, sometimes a joke, a story, when the audience cracks up, they think it's funny too, what happens is, the press will report it rather straight on, and it doesn't sound humorous at all. As a matter of fact, it sounds, sometimes it can sound not only inappropriate, but downright crass. That's happened to me a few times." Senator Conrad Burns was also wary about what the media might do to humor: "I think when you try to use humor with the press, very little of that is successful. I think that the general media people, reporters, are humorless. I don't think they ever do anything fun in their lives." Representative Schroeder commented about the difficulties of having C-SPAN ever present on the floor of Congress: "People just take themselves very, very seriously. And I think with C-SPAN and everything in there, there's a real hesitation. If you did anything that bombed, they would have it on tape and run it over and over and over, you know." Senator Dole conceded that the media might have a sense of humor but in a backhanded sort of way: "I must say, I've been criticized for a lot of things. It's not very often, because I've made people laugh. I mean even some of the worst people in the media laugh before they beat you up."

Senator Simpson had an especially up-and-down relationship with the press during his years in the Senate. When he first came to the Senate, the press received him favorably. "I suppose they considered me something of a novelty. My distinctly Western style—alarming nasal twang, odd vocal and facial expressions, earthy or even ribald sense of humor—apparently endeared me to a press corps that was accustomed to a much more buttoned-down crowd" (1997, 60–61). He was written up in the *Washington Post* as a "western breeze through the stuffy Senate," "A senator who finds renewal in Thurber and Mencken, keeps Western originals by Russell and Remington on his walls and sees the Senate as something of a funny farm deserves a closer look" (W. Sinclair 1980, A2; quoted in Simpson 1997, 61). However, when he used his humor in ways that were unpopular with much of the press establishment, such as with the Gulf War and especially with the Clarence Thomas hearings, he was the recipient of an ugly press. *Newsweek* ran an article about his fall from the Georgetown "A" social list. In happier days he was compared to Will Rogers, but "the days of Simpson Chic are over. He is now more often compared to Red-baiter Joseph McCarthy" (Clift 1991, 30). Further along in the same article, "'He's a real street fighter who masks it with a sense of humor,' says a Senate staffer. 'If Freud was right and humor is disguised hostility, Simpson is one angry man" (30). In the article, Simpson is quoted as saying he had been called "menacing, evil, bitter, foul, poophead" (30). It is as though once having been a favorite of the press, he fell from grace and was now singled out for especially vitriolic press comment—he was, as it were, a fallen wit. This might lead one to ask the question, Is there a special malevolence reserved for the humorist who is recast to seem duplicitous? Shortly after his retirement from the Senate, Simpson published his book *Right in the Old Gazoo* (1997), which was critical of the ways of the press and media.

IDEOLOGUES DON'T GET IT

A feeling runs deep among some of the congresspersons whom I interviewed that the ideologues in Congress, both Left and Right, don't get it. They do not understand the role of negotiation and play in forging the compromises that are so essential in accomplishing the work of a legislature. As they see it, no bread is better than the proverbial half-loaf of a Lyndon Johnson. Politics is truly a blood sport to them. They had changed the nature of the legislative endeavor so that it was not fun anymore for the humorists. There was no room for lightheartedness in the dour work of statecraft. If an effort was made to facilitate communication or reduce tension with a humorous remark or a story, they stare blankly at its source. They just do not understand. "In my party, if you try any compromise, you are a wimp. But you cannot legislate that way" (*Sunday Morning*, ABC, October 19, 1997). So declared Senator Simpson.

Representative Hefner also addressed the problem of ideologues.

> The new people that have come in the last cycle [104th Congress, 1995–1997] are just absolutely true ideologues. Most of them vote to the Far Right and some to the Far Left, but they really don't get it. . . . Nothing is humorous to them. Everything is serious. I remember I had a little skin cancer taken off my forehead. And the doctor put a little patch on it and my friend from Kentucky, who is a Republican from Kentucky, Mr. Rogers . . . got on an elevator and he said, "What's with the head bit?" I said, "Well, you know, Hal, we've got a problem we're going to have to cope with one of these days." I said, "I was leaving the other night, and I went in the parking lot and it was late." And I said, "One of those black helicopters came down, and they abducted me and they implanted a computer chip in my forehead where they will know exactly where I am at all times." And I said, "That's going to be a problem for us." He said, "For God's sakes, don't tell these new guys; they'll believe every word."

Senator Burns also believes that ideologues do not have a sense of humor. "You've also got to remember that sometimes folks just don't get it.

They don't understand it. And I've always felt sorry for those people. But nonetheless, you are going to have one or two who do not understand it. I like to talk about our family situation and some folks who are bent on a political agenda or some sort of an agenda and they just see no humor in anything. I've always felt sorry for those people."

Representative Hyde remembered an insight from a former member of Congress: "I've always loved the remark made by a former senator from New York, Roscoe Conkling, at the turn of the century. He said, 'But a lot of times people stare at you; they don't get it at first.' But it's a great line. He said that when Doctor Johnson said patriotism is the last refuge of the scoundrel, he never considered the possibilities of 'reform.' Well, that's a beautiful line. A lot of people look at you. They don't know what the hell you're talking about. But it's a marvelous line."

Senator Bumpers, who arrived with the class of 1974, had a long perspective on how the Senate has developed in recent years. "You can go along with great bipartisanship for a couple of months, and then suddenly there's a firestorm. You know, unforgiving, stridency, and partisanship." Does he think the Senate was more strident than in the past? "By light years."

CONCLUSION

Scholars of humor tell us that humor has to have a target, that it is combative, and that it is likely to represent a form of sublimated aggression. Recent studies of Congress point out that traditional norms facilitating work and civility among members have eroded, signaling the end of comity among members. Such findings lead us to believe that humor in Congress is aggressive, loaded with the freight of personal ridicule.

Not so, according to these legislative practitioners of political humor. Humor is seen by them as a way of ingratiating one's self with colleagues, of calling attention to one's message, and of humanizing the institution of Congress. If a member has a reputation for being especially witty, others will anxiously await his or her speech, in anticipation of something memorable. Sometimes creativity is enhanced, as when the unthinkable is uttered in the guise of comedic word play. Humor is perceived, then, as beneficial not only to the individuals who employ it, in terms of enhanced influence, but also to the institution of Congress, in terms of reducing tension and facilitating legislative work.

We can usefully think of the Capitol as a huge theater. The star performers, from our perspective, are a small troupe of humorists, comprising a half-dozen legislators, more or less. Some are storytellers, others quipsters. They know how to use language cleverly, to create incongruities of meaning, interruptions of logical thought, and so on. It is imaginative work, just as the art of forging great legislative compromises requires imagination. It is playful—it is the bringing of unlikely ideas together, like the similar process of searching for compromises. "If I say this or propose this, what will the target's reaction be, and in turn, how will I react?" The humorists are judged by the audience, and likewise they evaluate one another's performances. They learn from one another's mistakes and successes. They choose to use self-effacing humor because it carries with it the least risk. Ridicule has its place, but it is seen more as a defensive strategy to protect one's turf and save face. It carries a substantial risk. As they see it, the downside of employing humor is either that others might not take them seriously if they are too often seen as fishing for laughs or that their humor might detract from their message. As well, their humor might also be misunderstood. The media makes humor difficult, too, because when it reports on the work of the humorists, it leaves out the context, gestures, and emphases.

A significant and growing body of Congress at the time of this work were the ideologues of the Right and the Left, and they did not appreciate the role of humor in legislative affairs. For them, politics was a morality play: victory is won when their opposition has been exposed and driven from the stage. The humorists I interviewed found ideologues to be too rigid in their thinking. They believed that the ideologues needed to be more flexible and to engage in more play, as a way of enhancing their understanding and ferreting out compromise.

Though our humorists see humor as important to the work of Congress in the 1997–1998 period, when most of these interviews were conducted, these members nonetheless seem to long for a time when relations in Congress will again become kindlier and when wit and legislative play will be restored to a more readily accepted role in the affairs of the institution.

NOTES

1. The current and recent members who are interviewed include Representatives Barney Frank (D-MA), W. G. "Bill" Hefner (D-NC), Henry J. Hyde (R-IL), and Patricia Schroeder (D-CO); and Senators Dale Bumpers (D-AR), Conrad Burns (R-MT), Robert Dole (R-KS), Alan K. Simpson (R-WY), and Pat Roberts (R-KS). Congressman Frank was gracious enough to be interviewed twice: he was the first congressman interviewed, in October 1994, at which time I did not use a tape recorder; he agreed to be interviewed again in 1998, this time with a tape recorder, which I requested so that I could get comparable richness in quotations. In all cases except for Frank, in 1994, congresspersons were asked their permission to be

tape-recorded. In all cases, at the beginning of each interview, I asked that the comments be made for attribution. All taped interviews were by telephone except the one with Representative Schroeder.

Three of these members retired at the end of the 104th Congress: Representative Patricia Schroeder and Senators Simpson and Dole. The other six all continued on to the 105th Congress, during which time all but one of these interviews were conducted.

Our starting list of legislators to be interviewed included those I knew to have a reputation for using humor in their legislative work. In each interview, I inquired as to other legislators whom I might be overlooking. If two or more members mentioned a legislator not on the list, I contacted that legislator. In all, thirteen current and recent members were contacted, and ten agreed to be interviewed; one eventually did not give approval for the interview to be used for this book. This rate of participation shows the importance they attach to humor as a part of their legislative work.

2. One of the most noted instances in recent times of deflating pretension took place between two members of the Senate, the young Dan Quayle (R-IN) and the senior Lloyd Bentsen (D-TX), while they were running for vice president. Comparisons between the youthful Quayle and former president Kennedy came easily, and Quayle did not discourage them, different party affiliations notwithstanding. So when the topic of experience for the second-highest office came up in a televised debate, Quayle responded, "I have as much experience in the Congress, as Jack Kennedy did when he sought the Presidency." Delivering a knockout punch, the more senior Senator Bentsen responded, "Senator, I served with Jack Kennedy, I knew Jack Kennedy. Jack Kennedy was a friend of mine. Senator, you're no Jack Kennedy" (Dionne 1988, 1).

3. Representative Traficant (D-OH) was a maverick who was audacious in his use of humor. One of his most repeated lines was "Beam me up," which, as followers of *Star Trek* know, calls attention to the lack of intelligent life in the vicinity. Duncan and Lawrence (1997, 1195) counted that he had used this phrase more than ninety-five times in speeches during the 104th Congress. He also said that Congress was so dumb it could throw itself on the ground and miss, a comment not intended to ingratiate himself with other members (for this comment and a sampling of his humor, see Duncan and Lawrence 1997, 1158–60). He was a frequent user of the one-minute speech in Congress, and he often took this forum as an opportunity to craft policy statements with humorous content. His brassy humor often addressed issues such as the loss of jobs because of the globalization, his opposition to flag burning, the problem of illegal immigrants, the greed of HMO executives, and what he saw as the heavy-handedness and foolishness of government bureaucracies. Although it played well with his constituents back home, it did not work as well with members of Congress. In April 2002 Representative Traficant was convicted in federal court on multiple charges of bribery, racketeering, and tax evasion. In July of the same year he was expelled from Congress by a vote of 420–1, in the House of Representatives (Martinez 2002, 2036–37). The vote might suggest that humor does not necessarily work to ingratiate one with colleagues, but then ingratiating himself with other members of Congress was

never his purpose. It must also be noted that in a happier time in his career he was nonetheless recognized for his flair for theatrics and his outrageous humor. Published in the *Washingtonian* in September 2000, a poll of top congressional staff members of both parties voted Traficant the second-funniest member of the House, behind Barney Frank. He was also voted the top-ranked fashion victim and the third-biggest windbag in the House ("Best and Worst of Congress," 58–61).

Conclusion:
Keep 'em Laughin'

Senate, *n*. A body of elderly gentlemen charged with high duties and misdemeanors.

—Ambrose Bierce, *The Devil's Dictionary*

Humor has been an important part of Congress since the institution's inception. The lore of congressional humor runs the gamut, from the sharp-edged wit of John Randolph of Roanoke to the gentle, prodding wit of Mo Udall. As a good story is one that is retold, members of Congress regale one another by retelling humorous stories, changing the particulars to suit their needs, and sometimes attributing authorship of the stories to different members or former members. Indeed, plagiarism is an accepted practice where humor is concerned, and it is not uncommon for a member to retell a classic chestnut as though it was his or her own creation. While the stories are told with varying attributions as to authorship, they are often revealing as to what they say about the institution as well as the individual. So as members of Congress participate in the sharing of humor, they are also likely to be passing on a bit of shared congressional heritage.

TYPES OF HUMOR

One important strain of thought in the literature of humor in general, as well as in that of political humor, holds that humor is really sublimated aggression—that much of it consists of ridicule and that, to understand it, one need only know who is being ridiculed and why. Those of this persuasion contend that humor invariably has an aggressive edge and is a form of "social ragging." Typical depictions of Congress reinforce the expectation that congressional humor is acerbic. Characterizations such as the "legislative struggle," "legislative combat," and "legislative stalemate" suggest that congressional humor is of a rough-and-tumble nature, lending itself to ridicule, snappy comebacks, and clever put-downs. Thus, important themes both in the theory of humor and in the literature of legislative behavior lead us to anticipate that humor in Congress is of the superiority kind and that it has an aggressive edge, heavy with personal ridicule and aimed at vanquishing one's adversaries in policy encounters.

However, this is not what we found. Except for the very earliest decades in the history of Congress, incongruity humor and relief humor seem to be the preferred types of humor among members, based on autobiographies, books of noted congressional humorists, and congressional humor books in general. This conclusion was also borne out by our interviews with contemporary members of Congress who are noted for their use of humor. This might seem ironic, since one would expect that members of Congress who are successful acquirers of power would probably show a preference for superiority humor. How can we account for this?

In our society, it is a taboo to be too overtly interested in acquiring political power. Those who are successful in American politics are able to sublimate their interest in power and express it in terms either of espousing public policies that they identify as being in the public interest or in exhibiting an altruistic desire to serve the public good. In this milieu, to offer comments dripping with sarcasm and ridicule against opponents, even in a humorous vein, would be seen by the public as being mean-spirited, with its bearer unworthy of its trust. This is not to say that such sentiments are not expressed in comments offered in private among trusted friends. It is very likely that they abound away from the public's eyes and ears. However, in this study, because we have focused on the public humor of congressional elites, we have picked up only the slightest echoes of this private sarcasm. But, clearly, with reference to public congressional humor, the most sweeping claims of those who espouse the superiority theory of humor are not borne out.

Though there was a preference for the more playful kinds of humor—that is, incongruity and relief humor—this general observation begs for elaboration. For example, prevailing attitudes that change over time are important to the acceptability of humor. Thus, humor involving ridicule appears to be more pervasive in the nineteenth and early twentieth centuries than it has been since. But even among the most skilled practitioners of humor who were members of Congress during the nineteenth century, there seems to be a clear preference for clever and playful humor. This generalization holds even for persons widely known for their skill at ridicule, such as Samuel Cox. That being said, ridicule, though not preferred in the more recent decades, has continued to be seen as having its place. Even among twentieth-century members who clearly prefer playful humor, several understand that the occasional use of ridicule or sarcasm might be useful to protect one's self against the aggressiveness of others, to spark fear of one's self in an opponent, or to deflate the pretensions of an opponent.

What of vulnerability humor? We didn't even find this type, save perhaps indirectly in the trickster humor of Adam Clayton Powell, the flamboyant congressman from Harlem. This doesn't mean that it isn't important in political humor in general. However, as we have received humor through the lore of Congress, it seems that humor must have a human face—and this is an important point. Something of consequence is brought to a story when it is attributed to a particular current member or, perhaps even better, when it is about or attributed to a former member of Congress. Personal connection adds richness to a story; it brings to a humorous story the consideration of the member's stature and reputation in the institution. Then, too, we must point out that the attribution of humor is a form of flattery, a way for a person to ingratiate him- or herself with another. At the same time, members of Congress seek recognition and pride themselves in their verbal facility. The claim of authorship of humor is a bid for recognition of one's cleverness.

Of political humor in general, how typical is congressional humor? Though there are many similarities, there may also be important differences. In a political campaign, for example, the purpose is to defeat one's opponent and, in this sense, vanquish him or her. Once the election is over, one often has no further need to work closely with one's opponent, as in a legislature, so one may have more room to use superiority humor. Moreover, legislatures are likely to have institutional norms that prescribe a level of civility that inhibits the rougher forms of humor. However, even in political campaigns, prevailing norms of a society limit how far one can go in putting down an opponent. Meanness that is obviously gratuitous is likely to backfire. It may encourage revenge, which, if successful, will seem sweeter to the target, justified to the audience, and more humiliating to the perpetrator. And, of course, some topics are just likely to be seen as out-of-bounds humor.

POLITICAL CORRECTNESS—A MATTER OF CONTEXT

Attitudes about the appropriateness—now, the political correctness—of humor have varied greatly over time. For Samuel Cox, writing in the last quarter of the nineteenth century, any topic, *bar none*, was an appropriate target for political humor. He includes personal characteristics about people and physical peculiarities as appropriate subjects for humor. Representative Cox greatly admired ethnic humor and sectional humor, and he includes chapters about them in his book. In his time, humor celebrated the diversity of our country, and it did not have to be true. According to Cox, a distinctive characteristic of American humor is its propensity toward wild exaggeration.

His conception of good taste in humor is light years away from contemporary attitudes of political correctness, which severely circumscribe topics of contemporary humor. For contemporaries in Congress, practicing humor is like walking on eggshells—nay, walking through minefields. They approach humor cautiously, ever carrying a ready apology to smooth the ruffled feathers of the offended. Topics off-limits to them include jokes about race, gender, sexual orientation, ethnic groups, and religion; off-color jokes; the personal characteristics of others; their physical characteristics; jokes about their families; and so on. Senator Pat Roberts laments that the breadth of the proscribed topics is wide open—there are no fences. We might then raise the question, Has the pendulum on this topic swung too far toward limiting humor?

To shed some light on this question, we can look at the characteristics of humor, to begin to assess the need for narrowly circumscribing appropriate topics for humor. First, humor represents a reality of its own—an intrusion into the real world, if you will—similar to that of sleeping, magic, religion, and so on. This other reality is entered when the creator of humor sets the frame that what follows is not to be taken literally—for example, by communicating through verbal means or nonverbal gestures, or through a wink of the eye or a tone of the voice. This process of setting the frame tells all concerned that what follows is a kind of play and should be taken as such. Further, humor takes place within a particular context—that is, the values of a culture and the norms of an institution. What is being suggested here is that even without the stringent, overt restraints of political correctness, humor is bounded and cannot stray too far from contemporary standards. As Representative Barney Frank puts it, "If it's off-limits for serious conversation, it's off-limits for humor. Political humor doesn't give you license to say things that you couldn't otherwise say."

To further assess costs of contemporary ideas of political correctness, we need to ask, What kind of benefits does humor bring to legislative bodies? Humor represents a kind of play. By juxtaposing dissimilar ideas—even by thinking the unthinkable—it is possible that novel solutions might be found to heretofore intractable problems, which is one reason that the jester was tolerated in royal courts of yore. The jester told obvious truths which others dared not speak. Similarly, in a legislative setting, humor can ring a bell and bring a receptivity for messages that otherwise might not even receive consideration. A benefit often cited for humor is that it can be a way of cutting through tension. Whether in committees or on the floor, this ability to lessen tension can be important in bringing people together to facilitate legislative solutions. This aspect is even more important to reaching agreement in legislatures said to be stalemated, as with recent Congresses, than in more placid ones. Legislative compromise often requires the sort of creativity and play found in humor. The mental agility required for one is the same as that required for the other, so in this way the important process of legislative compromise can be enhanced through the toleration of humor and humorous people. It has been said that humor leavens human relationships. It can bridge chasms between individuals. If individuals of different political parties and factions can appreciate one another's humor, it can provide an island of trust that can lead to other kinds of interaction, some policy relevant.

Finally, humor is a source of group identification. It can be a way of solidifying one's own group. As well, drawing on ethnic humor or gender humor, so long as it is in good taste, can be a way of showing respect for another group and of demonstrating that one accepts the group's claims to legitimacy. It is ironic that, as we celebrate human diversity, humor about diversity must not be a part of that celebration. In nineteenth-century America, these ethnic differences were the source of much mirth, even national pride.

HUMOR AND SEEKING RECOGNITION AMONG EQUALS

Our congressional interviewees, as well as some of the earlier members (as referenced in their biographies and in congressional humor books), tend to agree that self-effacing humor is most likely the best form of humor. That such humor is likely to pass the political-correctness test surely contributes to this substantial agreement; that is, even if you can't poke fun of others, you can at least target yourself. Granted, this kind of humor can ingratiate one's self with an audience at an after-dinner speech or whatever by conveying the impression that a politician is just an ordinary, down-to-Earth sort of bloke, free of the all-too-common power hang-ups of politicians. Its appeal is no doubt strengthened by the skill with which President Reagan was able to poke fun at himself. Its usefulness seems to be greater, however, when congressional members meet the public than when they deal with their congressional colleagues. When one is working with peers in Congress, it is important to project the impression that one has command of relevant knowledge and possesses professional competence. Self-deprecating humor is of limited use here and, employed too often, might even mark one as a patsy—that is, one not to be taken seriously. Clever word play, ready quips, and skill in ferreting out incongruities are more likely to bring favorable attention to a congressional member in dealing with other members. The ability to consistently use humor to amplify a message, to work one's way out of tight spots, to reduce tensions, to tell timely stories, to deflate the ego of a rival—these are the stuff of legislative legends. And, impressions to the contrary notwithstanding, self-effacing humor is not what it seems. At base, it is a tactic of poking fun of one's self for the purpose of ingratiating one's self with others; so, in its own way, it is a power trip.

HUMOR AND SOCIAL DEFINITION

Social definition affects the availability of humor for use by individuals and groups. One congressional group that has suffered over much of its history because of the way it has been defined includes African American members. The image of African Americans that carried forward from the slavery period was that of the simpleton named Sambo. Sambo was a perpetually happy, ignorant buffoon, who was an everyman's slave on Southern plantations. He regaled massa with stories, he sang, he danced, and he had not a care or worry. He happily worked the cotton fields, and he and his family served massa in every way, answering every whim of the owners because the slaves were, after all, property. Since African American humor was integrally tied with the image of Sambo—which was a demeaning humor, designed to gain total control over slaves and total subservience from them—it made humor unavailable to former slaves and the ancestors of slaves who served in Congress. And these racial stereotypes did not end with slavery and Reconstruction. Though the racist humor of white members softened over time, blacks continued to be defined as ignorant and shiftless in racially humorous stories in the congressional humor lore through the first half of the twentieth century. Only after popular comedians ridiculed these stereotypes directly, through television and other media, was it safe for African American members to employ humor in their congressional communication. In Congress, where power is the coinage of exchange, attempts by black members to use this type of humor recalled old racist stereotypes and debased their currency. Sambo/slave humor, rich as it was, became dysfunctional for African American members in their congressional roles, though a distinctly black version of it continued to be ever present and popular in black culture. Indeed, until quite recently, it made the use of humor of any kind unavailable to them.

HUMOR AND CHANGE IN CONGRESS

One finds contradictory assertions in the literature of humor: on the one hand, humor favors the status quo; on the other, it is a change agent. Because of what we have seen in the congressional humor lore, we can safely accept both assertions. That is, many of the stories we find support existing norms in the Congress, while others auger for change. The most prolific relevant humor is subtle, and it gravitates toward supporting existing relationships or other approximate arrangements.

Another type of change humor, which we might call *maverick humor,* is likely to occur in relation to specific policies or amendments. This kind of humor is more opportunistic and often amounts to clowning around. It does little more than call attention to its author as a clever, albeit offbeat, person (though it should be said that that is no insignificant benefit). Huey Long and James Traficant might be cited as examples of those who use maverick humor.

Our third type of change humor is aimed at changing power relationships in a society by attacking fundamental policies. Humor of this kind is often jarring. The truth of the matter is that it is likely to require outrageous behavior or outlandish humor to challenge the icy silence that encapsulates taboo issues and keeps them from public consideration. Only through attention-getting behavior can the spectrum of issues thought to be appropriate for public discussion be broadened to include heretofore consensually excluded ones. Members who use humor in this way do not ingratiate themselves with contemporary members of Congress, but then that is not their main goal.

This type of humor was employed by two female members of Congress, Representatives Bella Abzug and Patricia Schroeder. They sought to fundamentally alter the treatment of women in our society, and they approached this task by advocating a broad range of gender issues: women's health, equality in the workplace, sufficient day care, medical leave, women's right to choice, and so on. They were also concerned with the House's rules (and how they affected female members), the fair allocation of facilities, and the culture of how to treat female staff members. The most notable aspect of their humor was the role that theater played in it. Theater was a serious affair to them, and they performed with much skill. Costumes, performances, and salty language, along with much humor, all were drawn on to focus attention on gender issues.

The behavior of Congressman Powell was also of this type of humor. He came to Congress from a Harlem district at a time when there was little reason to hope that he could form coalitions to pass civil rights legislation; so, he purposely made himself a "congressional irritant." He did this primarily through the use of trickster humor, which can be traced to slavery antecedents. As found in black culture, this humor involves the use of double meanings, irony, ambiguity, and (at times) lying and deceit— all of this in the interest of survival. Powell cut a dashing figure in Washington. Always sartorially attired, he drove a vintage Jaguar convertible and frequented the most exclusive restaurants, sometimes with white women on his arm. He played it loose with office and travel expenses and was ultimately denied a seat in the House by his colleagues, although he was subsequently reelected by an overwhelming majority. While his behavior scandalized white members of the House and some of his more educated black constituents, anecdotal evidence supports the conclusion that many of his poor constituents identified with his trickster behavior because it showed them that at least some blacks could stand up and lead a life of luxury as whites did. To criticism of his behavior, he simply responded that he would behave as other congressmen behaved. In effect, the image he intended to project was that as a black member of the House, he was equal to any other member, even in questionable behavior. In its way, that was a dramatic message, and it was delivered in a way consistent with an important strain of humor in black culture.

HUMOR AND THE ASSIMILATION OF NEW POPULATIONS

Institutions such as Congress must find ways to assimilate members who represent segments of the population not previously included. An important population to belatedly find representation in its halls is women. Defining new relationships between the sexes was awkward, and it took place over several decades. Much negotiation was required for this process, and humor played an important role.

From its creation, Congress had been an all-male fraternity, but beginning in 1917, as a result of suffragette activities, women began to show up on its rosters. The issues Congress had to confront were as broad as the question of equality of the sexes. How were female members to dress, and how were they to be addressed? Many of the new female members were widows who won appointment to finish the remainder of their deceased husbands' term; for male members, this raised the question of their legitimacy. Just how qualified were female members if they hadn't even been tempered in the heat of elections? And again, males worried that the women would narrowly focus on women's issues rather than take an interest in the broad spectrum of public policies that confronted Congress. For many male members, at base it was a question of whether women even belonged in Congress and whether they should be minding their homes and caring for their children.

Early suffragettes experienced anxiety as to whether female members would be accepted by male members and whether they would be treated fairly and with dignity. And no doubt about it—female congresspersons have been especially concerned with a broad range of gender-equality issues but also with the panoply of other issues to come before Congress. In addition, of special interest to female members were the fairness issues dealing with the management of Congress.

Male and female members alike had to participate in defining new relationships, which resulted in much uncertainty and fumbling. There were actions and reactions; female claims were followed by male put-downs; chauvinism was met with sarcasm. Humor—with its playfulness, ambiguity, and tentativeness—has been an important cushion throughout this assimilation process.

HUMOR AND HARD TIMES

Over the years, some members of Congress have developed reputations as skilled humorists. They have used humor in their legislative work and have benefited from doing so. Their preferred method of humor is the gentle, playful kind, involving quips, storytelling, ironies, word play, and so on. Ridicule and sarcasm, while they had their place, are not preferred. As important, they believe that humor brings with it important benefits to Congress that expedite work by reducing tensions and bringing members together. The representatives and senators whom I interviewed continue to hold onto these beliefs even though the time in which I interviewed them was one of congressional stalemate and partisan bickering (1997–1998). The level of tension within Congress was arguably the highest it had been during the twentieth century. Trust between members of opposite parties was uncharacteristically low, and the civility of past decades was noticeably lacking. These members continued to use humor but felt severely limited by the constraints of political correctness. Humor depends on context, and context depends on perspective. In this atmosphere, stories and quips can be given uncharitable meanings never intended by their authors. So here is the dilemma: Is it a characteristic of legislatures that when humor is most needed, it is least tolerated? If so, it is irony without humor.

Appendix

I employed a semistructured questionnaire to interview members of Congress who were identified as being noted for their use of humor. The goal in seeking these interviews was to allow the congresspersons' thoughts about humor to flow as freely as possible. At the same time, I wanted to query them about specific items. Thus, in each interview, I sought their reflections pertaining to the questions that follow. However, I also encouraged our interviewees to address topics of their own choosing at whatever length they were interested.

With a couple of exceptions, all interviews were via telephone, and all were tape-recorded (the exceptions are discussed in chapter 6, note 1). At the outset of each interview, permission was requested to tape-record our conversation, and I asked that the comments be for attribution. There were no objections. The telephone-interview technique was useful because it provided participants with flexibility. Their schedules were unpredictable, and when it became necessary to reschedule an interview, the author suffered no great inconvenience. Interviews could take place at a time of the participant's choosing, in the evening or in the morning, or during whenever time was available. A few of the interviews took place during the Christmas recess of 1997, while they were in their home districts and presumably less harried. Another important advantage of tape-recording the interviews was that doing so preserved the richness of the congresspersons' responses as they talked about humor.

QUESTIONS FOR CONGRESSIONAL HUMOR INTERVIEWS

1. What are the advantages of political humor for those who use it?

2. What are the dangers of political humor for those who use it?

3. What topics do you consider to be off-limits for political humor?

4. Can you think of examples of political humor by others that have worked well?

5. Can you think of examples of humor that fell flat or even backfired for others?

6. What do you think of the idea that jokes are always at someone's expense?

7. What actions, situations, or ingredients do you look for in creating political humor?

8. What interactions involving yourself are especially good examples of your political humor? Source and approximate date?

9. Can you think of examples of humor that fell flat or even backfired for you? Source and approximate date?

10. What are the contributions of political humor for Congress?

11. Do you have any sure formulas for political humor?

12. Do you have any favorite humorous political stories?

13. Have you written articles or books or granted published interviews that involve the topic of political humor? If so, where did they appear?

14. Characterize the likelihood of humor in each of the following circumstances.

    a. In congressional offices?

       very likely   not very likely
       somewhat likely   not at all likely
       likely

    b. On the floor during periods between floor consideration of issues?

       very likely   not very likely
       somewhat likely   not at all likely
       likely

c. During floor consideration of major issues?

very likely   not very likely
somewhat likely   not at all likely
likely

d. During floor consideration of minor issues?

very likely   not very likely
somewhat likely   not at all likely
likely

e. During committee/subcommittee deliberations?

very likely   not very likely
somewhat likely   not at all likely
likely

15. Can you suggest the names of others who are members of the House/Senate who use humor regularly in doing their work as members of Congress?

References

Abzug, Bella S. 1972. *Bella! Ms. Abzug Goes to Washington.* Edited by Mel Ziegler. New York: Saturday Review Press.

Auletta, Ken. 1975. "'Senator Bella'—Seriously." *New York Magazine*, August 11, 27–34.

Barkely, Alben W. 1954. *That Reminds Me.* New York: Doubleday.

Benner, Marie. 1977. "What Makes Bella Run?" *New York Magazine*, June 20, 54–64.

Berger, Arthur Asa. 1993. *An Anatomy of Humor.* New Brunswick, N.J.: Transaction Publishers.

———. 1995. *Blind Men and Elephants: Perspectives on Humor.* New Brunswick, N.J.: Transaction Publishers.

———. 1996. "The Politics of Laughter." In *The Social Faces of Humour: Practices and Issues,* edited by George E. C. Paton, Chris Powell, and Stephen Wagg. Aldershot, England: Arena.

Berger, Jerry. 2002. "Carnahan Draws Fire for Saying Bush Team Can't Get Bin Laden, so It's Going after Her." *St. Louis Post Dispatch*, October 16, A2.

Berger, Peter. 1997. *Redeeming Laughter.* New York: Walter De Gruyter.

Bergson, Henri. [1900] 1956. "Laughter." In *Comedy,* by Wylie Sypher. Baltimore: Johns Hopkins University Press.

Berlyne, D. E. 1969. "Laughter, Humor and Play." In *The Handbook of Social Psychology,* edited by Gardner Lindzey and Elliot Aronson. 2nd ed., vol. 3. Reading, Mass.: Addison Wesley, 795–852.

"Best and Worst of Congress." 2000. *Washingtonian* (September): 58–61.

Bierce, Ambrose. [1911] 1993. *The Devil's Dictionary.* New York: Dover.

Boller, Paul F., Jr. 1992. *Congressional Anecdotes.* New York: Oxford University Press.

Boskin, Joseph. 1971. "The Life and Death of Sambo." *Journal of Popular Culture* 4 (spring): 646–57.

————. 1986. *Sambo*. New York: Oxford University Press.

Boskin, Joseph, and Joseph Dorinson. 1987. "Ethnic Humor: Subversion and Survival." In *American Humor,* by Arthur Power Dudden. New York: Oxford University Press, 97–117.

Botkin, B. A. 1944. "The Slave as His Own Interpreter." *The Library of Congress Quarterly Journal of Acquisitions* 2 (July/September): 37–63.

Boykin, Edward, ed. 1961. *The Wit and Wisdom of Congress*. New York: Funk & Wagnalls.

Bradney, Pamela. 1957. "The Joking Relationship in Industry." *Human Relations* 10, no. 2: 179–87.

Clark, Champ. 1920. *My Quarter Century of American Politics*. Vol. 2. New York: Harper & Brothers.

Clift, Eleanor. 1991. "Taking the Low Road." *Newsweek,* October 28, 30.

Combs, James E., and Dan Nimmo. 1996. *The Comedy of Democracy.* Westport, Conn.: Praeger.

Coser, Rose Laub. 1960. "Laughter among Colleagues: A Study of the Social Functions of Humor among the Staff of a Mental Hospital." *Psychiatry* 23 (February): 81–95.

Cowan, William Tynes. 2001. "Plantation Comic Modes." *Humor: International Journal of Humor Research* 14, no. 1: 1–24.

Cox, Samuel S. [1880] 1969. *Why We Laugh*. New York: Benjamin Blom.

Dance, Daryl Cumber. 1978. *Shuckin' and Jivin': Folklore from Contemporary Black Americans*. Bloomington: Indiana University Press.

Davis, Murray S. 1993. *What's So Funny*. Chicago: University of Chicago Press.

Dionne, E. J., Jr. 1988. "Bentsen and Quayle Attack on Question of Competence to Serve in the Presidency." *New York Times*, October 6, 1.

Dorinson, Joseph, and Joseph Boskin. 1988. "Racial and Ethnic Humor." In *Humor in America: A Research Guide to Genres and Topics,* edited by Lawrence E. Mintz. New York: Greenwood Press.

Douglas, Mary. 1975. "Jokes." In *Implicit Meanings: Essays in Anthropology*. London: Routledge & Paul Keagan, 90–114.

Dowd, Maureen. 1998. "Joker McCain Really Goofed This Time." *Kansas City Star,* June 23, B7.

Dreifus, Claudia. 1972. "Women in Politics: An Interview with Edith Green." *Social Policy* 2 (January/February): 16–22.

Duncan, Philip D., and Christine C. Lawrence. 1997. *Politics in America 1998: The 105th Congress*. Washington, D.C.: Congressional Quarterly Press.

Dunne, Finley Peter. [1906] 1969. *Dissertations by Mr. Dooley*. Upper Saddle River, N.J.: Literature House/Gregg Press.

Eckardt, A. Roy. 1992. *Sitting in the Earth and Laughing: A Handbook of Humor*. New Brunswick, N.J.: Transaction Publishers

Ehrenhalt, Alan. 1982. "In the Senate of the '80s, Team Spirit Has Given Way to the Rule of Individuals." *Congressional Quarterly Weekly Report*, September 4, 2175–82.

Emerson, Joan P. 1969. "Negotiating the Serious Import of Humor. *Sociometry* 32 (June): 169–81.

Ervin, Sam J., Jr. 1983. *Humor of a Country Lawyer*. Chapel Hill: University of North Carolina Press.

Fadiman, Clifton, ed. 1985. *The Little, Brown Book of Anecdotes*. Boston, Mass.: Little, Brown.

Fine, Gary Alan. 1983. "Sociological Approaches to the Study of Humor." In *Handbook of Humor Research*, edited by Paul E. McGhee and Jeffry H. Goldstein. Vol. 1. New York: Springer-Verlag.

Freud, Sigmund. [1905] 1960. *Jokes and Their Relation to the Unconscious*. Translated and edited by James Strachey. New York: W.W. Norton.

Fry, William F. 1963. *Sweet Madness: A Study of Humor*. Palo Alto, Calif.: Pacific Books.

———. 1987. "Humor and Paradox." *American Behavioral Scientist* 30 (January/February): 42–71.

Gates, Henry Louis, Jr. 1988. *The Signifying Monkey: A Theory of Afro-American Literary Criticism*. New York: Oxford University Press.

Gertzog, Irwin N. 1995. *Congressional Women: Their Recruitment, Integration, and Behavior*. 2nd ed. Westport, Conn.: Praeger.

Gilfond, Duff. 1929. "Gentlewomen of the House." *American Mercury* (October): 151–61.

Gingras, Angele de T. 1973. *From Bussing to Bugging: The Best in Congressional Humor*. Washington, D.C.: Acropolis Books Limited.

Goffman, Erving. 1959. *The Presentation of Self in Everyday Society*. Garden City, N.J.: Doubleday Anchor Books.

Greenfield, Jeff. 1980. *Playing to Win*. New York: Simon and Schuster.

Gruner, Charles, R. 1978. *Understanding Laughter: The Workings of Wit and Humor*. Chicago: Nelson-Hall.

———. 1997. *The Game of Humor: A Comprehensive Theory of Why We Laugh*. New Brunswick, N.J.: Transaction Publishers.

Hamilton, Charles V. 1991. *Adam Clayton Powell, Jr.: The Political Biography of an American Dilemma*. New York: Atheneum.

Hanser, Richard. 1952. "Wit as a Weapon." *Saturday Review* 35:13–14, 51.

Haskins, James. 1977. *Barbara Jordan*. New York: Dial Press.

Harris, Leon A. 1964. *The Fine Art of Political Wit*. New York: E. P. Dutton.

Hays, Brooks. 1968. *A Hotbed of Tranquility*. New York: Macmillan.

Heller, Joseph. [1955] 1961. *Catch-22*. New York: Dell.

Hertzler, Joyce O. 1970. *Laughter: A Socio-Scientific Analysis*. New York: Exposition Press.

Hickey, Neil, and Ed Edwin. 1965. *Adam Clayton Powell and the Politics of Race*. New York: Fleet Publishing.

Hobbes, Thomas. [1640] 1969. *The Elements of Law: Natural and Politic*. Edited by Ferdinand Tonnes, with preface and critical notes (orig. 1889). New York: Barnes & Noble.

———. [1651] 1991. *Leviathan*. Edited by Richard Tuck. New York: Cambridge University Press.

Hogan, Bill, and Mike Hill. 1987. *Will the Gentleman Yield?* Berkeley, Calif.: Ten Speed Press.

Hughes, Langston, ed. 1966. *The Book of Negro Humor*. New York: Dodd, Meade.

Huitt, Ralph K. 1957. "The Morse Committee Assignment Controversy: A Study in Senate Norms." *American Political Science Review* 51 (June): 313–29.

———. 1961. "The Outsider in the Senate: An Alternative Role." *American Political Science Review* 55 (September): 566–75.

Hummel, Ralph P. 1991. "Stories Managers Tell: Why They Are Valid as Science." *Public Administration Review* 51 (January/February): 31–41.

Kassebaum, Nancy Landon. 1988. "The Senate Is Not in Order." *Washington Post*, January 27, A19.

Kenworthy, E. W. 1969. "A Political Phenomenon." *New York Times*, September 8, 26.

Kirkpatrick, Jeanne J. 1974. *Political Woman*. New York: Basic Books.

Klein, Joe, and Thomas Rosenstiel. 1995. "Mr. Inside." *Newsweek*, November 27, 32.

Koestler, Arthur. [1964] 1989. *The Act of Creation*. London: Arkana.

———. 1997. "Humour and Wit." In *The New Encyclopedia Britannica*. 15th ed., vol. 20, 682–88.

Levine, Lawrence W. 1977. *Black Culture and Black Consciousness: Afro-American Folk Thought from Slavery to Freedom*. New York: Oxford University Press.

Lundberg, Craig C. 1969. "Person-Focused Joking: Pattern and Function." *Human Organization* 28 (spring): 22–28.

MacNeil, Neil. 1970. *Dirksen: Portrait of a Public Man*. New York: World Publishing.

Mannies, Jo. 2002. "Carnahan Apologizes for Comment about Bush." *St. Louis Post-Dispatch*, October 17, A2.

March, James G., and Johan Olsen. 1989. *Rediscovering Institutions*. New York: Free Press.

Martin, Joanne. 1992. *Cultures in Organizations: Three Perspectives*. New York: Oxford University Press.

Martin, Joanne, and Melanie E. Powers. 1983. "Truth or Corporate Propaganda: The Value of a Good War Story." In *Organizational Symbolism*, edited by Louis R. Pondy, Peter J. Frost, Gareth Morgan, and Thomas C. Dandridge. Greenwich, Conn.: JAI Press, 93–107.

Martineau, William H. 1972. "A Model of the Social Functions of Humor." In *The Psychology of Humor: Theoretical Perspectives and Empirical Issues,* edited by Jeffrey H. Goldstein and Paul E. McGhee. New York: Academic Press, 101–25.

Martinez, Gebe. 2002. "Traficant's Ouster Decided but Not Relished by His Peers." *Congressional Quarterly Weekly Report* 60, no. 30 (July 27): 2036–37.

Matthews, Donald R. 1959. "The Folkways of the United States Senate: Conformity to Group Norms and Legislative Effectiveness." *American Political Science Review* 53 (December): 1064–89.

———. 1960. *U.S. Senators and Their World*. New York: Vintage Books.

Mead, George Herbert. [1934] 1962. *Mind, Self and Society*. Edited by, and with an introduction by, Charles W. Morris. Chicago: University of Chicago Press.

Merriam, Charles E. 1926. "Progress in Political Research." *American Political Science Review* 20 (February): 1–13.

Meyer, John W., and Brian Rowan. 1977. "Institutionalized Organizations: Formal Structure as Myth and Ceremony." *American Journal of Sociology* 83, no. 2: 340–63.

Miller, William "Fishbait." 1977. *Fishbait: The Memoirs of the Congressional Doorkeeper*. As told to Frances Spatz Leighton. Englewood Cliffs, N.J.: Prentice-Hall.

Mintz, Lawrence E., ed. 1988. *Humor in America: A Research Guide to Genres and Topics*. New York: Greenwood Press.

Mitroff, Ian I., and Ralph Kilmann. 1975. "Stories Managers Tell: A New Tool for Organizational Problem Solving." *Management Review* 64 (July): 18–28.

Mnookin, Seth. 2002. "Do the Traficant Rant." *Newsweek*, August 5, 29.

Morreall, John, ed. 1987. *The Philosophy of Laughter and Humor*. Albany: State University of New York Press.

Myrdal, Gunnar. 1944. *An American Dilemma: The Negro Problem and Modern Democracy*. Vol. 1. New York: Harper and Brothers Publishers.

Nilsen, Alleen Pace, and Don L. F. Nilsen. 2000. *Encyclopedia of Twentieth-Century American Humor*. Phoenix, Ariz.: Oryx.

Obrdlik, Antonin J. 1942. "Gallows Humor: A Sociological Phenomenon." *American Journal of Sociology* 47 (March): 709–16.

Olav, Hans, and Tor Myklebust. 1942. *He Who Laughs . . . Lasts: Anecdotes from Norway's Homefront*. Brooklyn, N.Y.: Norwegian News Company.

O'Neal, F. Hodge, and Ann Laurie O'Neal. 1964. *Humor: The Politician's Tool*. New York: Vantage.

Ornstein, Norman J., Robert L. Peabody, and David Rohde. 1977. "The Changing Senate: From the 1950s to the 1970s." In *Congress Reconsidered*, edited by Lawrence Dodd and Bruce Oppenheimer. New York: Praeger, 3–20.

———. 1985. "The Senate through the 1980s: Cycles of Change." In *Congress Reconsidered*, edited by Lawrence Dodd and Bruce Oppenheimer. Washington, D.C.: Congressional Quarterly Press, 13–33.

Osofsky, Gilbert, ed. 1969. *Puttin' on Ole Massa*. New York: Harper and Row.

Ott, Steven J. 1989. *The Organizational Culture Perspective*. Pacific Grove, Calif.: Brooks/Cole.

Parker, Robert. 1986. *Capitol Hill in Black and White*. New York: Dodd, Mead.

Powell, Adam Clayton. [1971] 1994. *Adam by Adam: The Autobiography of Adam Clayton Powell, Jr.* New York: Citadel Press.

Powell, Chris. 1988. "A Phenomenological Analysis of Humour in Society." In *Humour in Society: Resistance and Control*, edited by Chris Powell and George E. C. Paton. New York: St. Martin's Press, 86–105.

Powell, Chris, and George E. C. Paton, eds. 1988. *Humour in Society: Resistance and Control*. New York: St. Martin's Press.

Provine, Robert R. 2000. *Laughter: A Scientific Investigation*. New York: Viking.

Robbins, William. 1976. "Butz Quits under Fire amid Rising Protests about Racist Remark." *New York Times*, October 5, 1, 32.

Roberts, Steven V. 1984. "Senate's New Breed Shuns Novice Role." *New York Times*, November 26, A1, A18.

Schroeder, Pat. 1997. "New Solutions for a New Century." The Lloyd B. Thomas Lecture and Performance Series. University of Missouri, Columbia, February 17.

———. 1998. *24 Years of House Work and the Place Is Still a Mess*. Kansas City, Mo.: Andrews McMeel Publishing.

Schutz, Charles E. 1977a. *Political Humor: From Aristophanes to Sam Ervin*. Cranbury, N.J.: Associated University Presses.

———. 1977b. "The Psycho-logic of Political Humor." In *It's a Funny Thing, Humour*, edited by Anthony J. Chapman and Hugh C. Foot. New York: Pergamon Press.

"Sen. Packwood Resigns in Disgrace." 1995. *Congressional Quarterly Almanac* 51, ch. 1: 47–52.

Shabecoff, Philip. 1983. "Watt Battled a Rising Tide." *New York Times*, October 10, 1, 10.

Shadegg, Stephen. 1970. *Clare Boothe Luce.* New York: Simon and Schuster.

Shields, Mark. 1987. "Political Humor: Who Are All These Jokers?" *Public Opinion* 3 (September/October): 15–17, 57.

Simpson, Alan K. 1997. *Right in the Old Gazoo.* New York: William Morrow.

Sinclair, Barbara. 1989. *The Transformation of the U.S. Senate.* Baltimore, Md.: Johns Hopkins University Press.

Sinclair, Ward. 1980. "Freshman Simpson: Western Breeze through Stuffy Senate." *Washington Post*, January 22, A2.

Solomon, John. 1998. "Top 10 Funniest Politicians." *George*, August 8, 1998.

Stephenson, Richard M. 1951. "Conflict and Control Functions of Humor." *American Journal of Sociology* 56 (May): 569–74.

Sterling, Bryan. [1979] 2000. *The Best of Will Rogers.* New York: M. Evans.

Stokker, Kathleen. 1995. *Folklore Fights the Nazis: Humor in Occupied Norway, 1940–1945.* Madison: University of Wisconsin Press.

Swain, Carol M. 1993. *Black Faces, Black Interests.* Cambridge, Mass.: Harvard University Press.

"Tower Nomination Spurned by Senate." 1989. *Congressional Quarterly Almanac* 45: 403–13.

Traylor, Gary. 1985. "Joking in a Bush Camp." *Human Relations* 26 (August): 479–86.

Twain, Mark. 1899. *Following the Equator: A Journey Around the World.* Vol. 1. New York: Harper & Brothers.

Udall, Morris K. 1988. *Too Funny to be President.* New York: Henry Holt.

Uslaner, Eric M. 1993. *The Decline of Comity in Congress.* Ann Arbor: University of Michigan Press.

Victor, Kirk. 1998. "A Chink in McCain's Teflon." *National Journal* 26 (June 27): 1508–9.

Ward, Artemus [Charles Farrar Browne]. 1922. *The Complete Works of Artemus Ward.* London: Chatto & Windus.

Watson, James E. 1936. *As I Knew Them.* Indianapolis, Ind.: Bobbs-Merrill.

Webb, Ronald G. 1981. "Political Uses of Humor." *Et cetera* 38 (spring): 35–50.

White, William S. 1956. *Citadel: The Story of the U.S. Senate.* New York: Harper & Brothers.

Wiley, Alexander. 1947. *Laughing with Congress.* New York: Crown Publishers.

Wilkins, Alan L. 1983. "Organizational Stories as Symbols Which Control the Organization." In *Organizational Symbolism*, edited by Louis R. Pondy, Peter J. Frost, Gareth Morgan, and Thomas C. Dandridge. Greenwich, Conn.: JAI Press, 81–92.

Wilson, James Q. 1960. "Two Negro Politicians: An Interpretation." *Midwest Journal of Political Science* 4 (November): 346–69.

Yarwood, Dean L. 1981. "Oversight of Presidential Funds by the Appropriations Committees: Learning from the Watergate Crisis." *Administration and Society* 13 (November): 299–346.

———. 1993. "The Federalist Authors and the Problem of Equality between the Branches: A Study in Institutional Development." *Social Science Quarterly* 74 (September): 645–63.

———. 1995. "Humor and Administration: A Serious Inquiry into Unofficial Communication." *Public Administration Review* 55 (January/February): 81–90.

———. 2001. "When Congress Makes a Joke: Congressional Humor as Serious and Purposeful Communication." *Humor: International Journal of Humor Research* 14, no. 4: 359–94.

———. 2003. "Humorous Stories and the Identification of Senate Norms." *Administration and Society* 35 (March): 9–28.

Young, Stephen M. 1964. *Tales Out of Congress*. Philadelphia: J. B. Lippincott.

Zijderveld, Anton C. 1983. "The Sociology of Laughter and Humor." *Current Sociology* 31 (winter): 1–103.

PERSONAL INTERVIEWS

U.S. Representatives

Frank, Barney. 1994. Telephone interview, October 12.
———. 1998. Taped telephone interview, January 26.
Hefner, W. G. "Bill." 1997. Taped telephone interview, December 15.
Hyde, Henry. 1998. Taped telephone interview, January 13.
Schroeder, Patricia. 1997. Taped personal interview, February 17.

U.S. Senators

Bumpers, Dale. 1997. Taped telephone interview, October 1.
Burns, Conrad. 1997. Taped telephone interview, August 28.
Dole, Robert. 1997. Taped telephone interview, December 17.
Roberts, Pat. 1998. Taped telephone interview, February 2.
Simpson, Alan K. 1997. Taped telephone interview, May 2.

Index

151

About the Author

Dean L. Yarwood is professor emeritus at the University of Missouri, Columbia. He received his doctorate from the University of Illinois. He has been a faculty member at Coe College, the University of Kentucky, and the University of Missouri, Columbia. At Missouri, he served as chair of the political science department and was the Frederick A. Middlebush Professor in Political Science from 1992 to 1995. He is the author of numerous articles and is the editor of *The National Administrative System* and *Public Administration, Politics, and the People.* His current research interest is the role of humor in political communication, particularly in congressional and administrative communication.